ARTIFICIAL BEHAVIOR

Computer
Simulation
of Psychological
Processes

Prentice-Hall Personal Computing Series
Lance A. Leventhal, series editor

Anderson & Anderson, *The Unix C Shell Field Guide*
Busch, *Sorry About the Explosion: A Humorous Guide to Computers*
Dickey, *Kids Travel on Commodore 64*
Fabbri, *Animation, Games, and Graphics for the Timex-1000*
Fabbri, *Animation, Games, and Sound for the Apple II/IIe*
Fabbri, *Animation, Games, and Sound for the Commodore 64*
Fabbri, *Animation, Games, and Sound for the IBM PC*
Fabbri, *Animation, Games, and Sound for the TI 99/4A*
Fabbri, *Animation, Games, and Sound for the VIC 20*
Glazer, *Managing Money with Your Commodore 64*
Glazer, *Managing Money with Your IBM PC*
Glazer, *Managing Money with Your VIC 20*
Harris & Scofield, *IBM PC Conversion Handbook of BASIC*
Lima, *dBASE II for Beginners*
Lima, *Mastering dBASE III in Less Than a Day*
McLaughlin & Boulding, *Financial Management with Lotus® 1-2-3®*
Nitz, *Business Analysis and Graphics with Lotus® 1-2-3®*
Royer, *Handbook for Software and Hardware Interfacing for IBM PCs*
Scanlon, *EasyWriter II System Made Easy-er*
Scanlon, *Microsoft Word for the IBM PC*
Scanlon, *The IBM PC Made Easy*
Schnapp, *Macintosh Graphics in Modula-2*
Schnapp & Stafford, *Commodore 64 Computer Graphics Toolbox*
Schnapp & Stafford, *Computer Graphics for the Timex 1000 and Sinclair ZX-81*
Schnapp & Stafford, *VIC 20 Computer Graphics Toolbox*
Steinhauer, *Artificial Behavior: Computer Simulation of Psychological Processes*
Thro, *Making Friends with Apple Writer II*

ARTIFICIAL BEHAVIOR

Computer Simulation of Psychological Processes

Gene D. Steinhauer

Prentice-Hall
Englewood Cliffs, New Jersey 07632

Library of Congress Cataloging-in-Publication Data

Steinhauer, Gene D.
  Artificial behavior.

  (Prentice-Hall personal computing series)
  Includes bibliographies and index.
  1. Psychology—Data processing. 2. Psychology—
Simulation methods. 3. Computer simulation. 4. BASIC
(Computer program language) I. Title. II. Series.
BF39.5.S74 1986   150   86–4891
ISBN 0-13-048844-5

Editorial/production supervision: **Lisa Schulz**
Cover design: **Ben Santora**
Manufacturing buyer: **Gordon Osbourne**

© 1986 by Prentice-Hall
A Division of Simon & Schuster, Inc.
Englewood Cliffs, New Jersey 07632

The author and publisher of this book have used their best efforts in preparing this book. These efforts include the development, research, and testing of the theories and programs to determine their effectiveness. The author and publisher make no warranty of any kind, expressed or implied, with regard to these programs or the documentation contained in this book. The author and publisher shall not be liable in any event for incidental or consequential damages in connection with, or arising out of, the furnishing, performance, or use of these programs.

Printed in the United States of America

10 9 8 7 6 5 4 3 2 1

ISBN   0-13-048844-5   025

Prentice-Hall International (UK) Limited, *London*
Prentice-Hall of Australia Pty. Limited, *Sydney*
Prentice-Hall Canada Inc., *Toronto*
Prentice-Hall Hispanoamericana, S.A., *Mexico*
Prentice-Hall of India Private Limited, *New Delhi*
Prentice-Hall of Japan, Inc., *Tokyo*
Prentice-Hall of Southeast Asia Pte. Ltd., *Singapore*
Editora Prentice-Hall do Brasil, Ltda., *Rio de Janeiro*
Whitehall Books Limited, *Wellington, New Zealand*

CONTENTS

PREFACE

This book contains eight interactive, animated graphics, computer simulations of living organisms and the psychological knowledge on which they are based. The behavior of the simulated individuals depend on other screen events you control by keyboard inputs. All of these programs are written in APPLESOFT BASIC and will run on any of the members of the APPLE II family of computers. The programs can be typed into your computer from the listings in the text, stored to tape or disk, and executed. All of these programs have been used for classroom instruction or research purposes. They are written in a structured format to help you understand how they work. As written, these programs will not run over into the high resolution graphics memory and destroy the graphics display. If you wish to modify the programs, however, some knowledge of memory management, graphics animation, and machine language is essential.

The programs are written in BASIC to make them understandable by the largest possible audience. BASIC is now more widely used than any other programming language. The programs can, of course, be faster and/or more efficient using other computer languages. I encourage readers to attempt such translations. The same is true for the graphics and animation routines. They are written in the simplest form and can be made more efficient using other programming techniques. The psychological models I have used fit the largest amount of research data. Alternatives are available and can be easily substituted in these programs. Again, I encourage you to try alternative psychological models. Ultimately, however, most applications must use those formulations which fit our scientific knowledge.

The field of computer simulation of behavior has been very slow to develop. I have found it particularly difficult to write this book because I wanted it to be readable by a wide audience of computer scientists, educators, computer programmers, psychologists, students, and just about anyone who is interested in computers and psychology. Some chapters can be read with ease. Other chapters are necessarily more difficult. Now you have two vehicles to learn from, the book and the computer programs.

The text may contain new terms, or new definitions of familiar words. You will find definitions of those terms in the glossary at the back of the book. For those wishing more in depth treatment of the topics in each chapter, I have provided a list of additional readings at the end of each chapter.

ACKNOWL-EDGMENTS

My interest in computer simulation of psychological processes was encouraged by the results of an efficacy study of educational simulation I conducted at the State University of New York, College at Oswego, during the 1977–1978 academic year. That project was funded by the National Science Foundation's program, Comprehensive Assistance for Undergraduate Science Education (NSF, CAUSE). I gratefully acknowledge the contribution NSF and the psychology department faculty at SUNY, Oswego made to my interest in computer simulation. Throughout the development of these programs, and this book, I was fortunate to have support, encouragement, and feedback from many people. The development and testing of these programs spanned six years. Such a long and arduous effort could never have been

My ideas for Artificial Behavior were constantly encouraged by Blaine Peden, Helen Daly, and John Daly. Christopher W. Steinhauer and Steven P. Steinhauer, did some of the early graphics work for programs RAT 1 and PIGEON 1. Their efforts are gratefully acknowledged. While writing this book Andrew Simmons, Allen Skei, and Lance Leventhal prodded me to translate the highly refined language of laboratory research into words that were meaningful to a wider audience. I resisted their efforts almost every step of the way. In the end, I have tried to maintain the exactness of laboratory language in my use of everyday words. The contributions of Drs. Simmons, Skei, and Leventhal are gratefully acknowledged. Anne Sluis did the tedious work of proof reading the transcription of computer listings into text format. All of these people also read all or parts of the manuscript and provided excellent comments and reviews. Larry Berger, and the Psychology Department at the University of Montana, provided a pleasant and supportive environment in which the final draft of the book was completed. To all of these people I extend my sincere appreciation for their contributions, support, and encouragement.

Gene D. Steinhauer
Fresno, California

ARTIFICIAL BEHAVIOR

Computer Simulation of Psychological Processes

1

INTRODUCTION TO ARTIFICIAL BEHAVIOR

Imagine a computer game with animated characters displayed on the screen. The game player cannot control the characters directly, but he or she can control other parts of the screen display. The screen shows a front view of a typical family home. At one point in the game, the player presses a key that closes the garage door. The animated character who always found the garage door open in the past now finds it closed. The character frowns, mumbles under his breath, and kicks at the door. He is frustrated.

Imagine next a computer saying that it is disappointed because its owner only used it thirty minutes on bowling nights. Imagine the computer saying, "I trust you, but not your friends." Imagine a computer that teaches self-control and tells users when they are jealous. Envision a computer that becomes superstitious or depressed, a computer that learns courage, fear, persistence, and acquires concepts—a computer that shows hope.

Such a machine has long been the dream of science-fiction writers, computer magazine columnists, film directors, and sophomore electrical engineering students. But is such a computer destined to remain nothing more than a fantasy? No! Such a machine is a very real possibility. This book will introduce some techniques that will allow programmers to begin developing computers that mimic many human psychological states.

Experienced computer scientists have already created computers that behave as file clerks, jet aircraft pilots, accountants, psychotherapists, medical diagnosticians, and chess players. These simulations, programs that behave as if they are humans, have been developed using a well-established pattern of research. First, the computer scientist describes the tasks and goals of some human activity, such as playing chess. That description includes the layout of the chess board, and the scientist defines the goals as capturing the opponent's pieces. Second, he observes a person playing chess, and he looks for regular patterns of behavior. In the case of a chess player, the computer scientist might see the player frequently pausing to consider every possible move and its consequences in terms of the opponent's subsequent moves. Third, using this information, the programmer writes a set of instructions giving the computer the task description (board layout, rules for moving pieces), the goals (capture opponent's pieces), and the rule developed by watching the human play chess (entertain each possible move and its consequences). The computer is then pitted against human players, the computer's skill is observed, and the program is refined again and again. This sequence of activity for developing computer simulations of human behavior is outlined in Figure 1-1.

The pattern of research shown in Figure 1-1 was used by computer programmers to develop chess programs that defeat all but a small number of

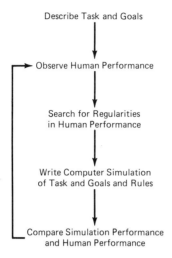

Figure 1-1. Five general steps in developing Artificial Intelligence and Artificial Behavior computer programs. Steps 2 through 5 define a loop that is repeated until the computer functions at some predefined level of accuracy.

the world's best players. Yet a computer that plays chess—no matter how intelligent it appears to be—is far different from a computer that demonstrates psychological states such as expectations, frustration, and courage.

ARTIFICIAL BEHAVIOR AND ARTIFICIAL INTELLIGENCE

Chess-playing computer programs, medical diagnosis programs, and other expert systems have been developed by people working in the academic field of Artificial Intelligence (AI). The goal of researchers in AI is to create programs that mimic or simulate intelligent human behavior. Success in this effort depends on the researchers finding rules describing what humans do when playing chess, flying a jet, diagnosing illnesses, or performing other intelligent activities.

A computer is governed by rules at each level of operation. Rules for counting, adding, subtracting, multiplying, and dividing using a binary number system (0 and 1) allowed us to develop electronic switching devices to perform ordinary arithmetic. Electronic calculators are the everyday product developed from those rules. A set of rules that symbolize letters of the alphabet in electronic switching circuits (ASCII code) makes it possible to write, edit, and print using word processors. The success of all computer applications, including Artificial Intelligence, depends on finding and using a set of rules.

In order to develop computers, or computer programs, that demonstrate some of the psychological states mentioned in the opening paragraphs (frustration, disappointment, cooperation, self-control, etc.), we must have a set of rules. For example, one thing we can do is look for such rules in the literature of behavioral science. The rules need not be perfect when we begin our quest for humanlike computers. We only need a start. Many AI applications are being constantly improved by starting with imperfect rules and repeating the loop diagrammed in Figure 1-1.

Those who believe that human beings are too complicated and flexible to be represented by a set of rules will be surprised to learn that many formal models of human behavior do exist. The behavioral science literature contains numerous rules for describing human emotions, reason, and expression.

I will use the term *Artificial Behavior (AB)* to refer to the use of rules about psychological processes in animated graphics simulations, computer operating systems, and robotics. The emphasis in Artificial Behavior is on the representation of the computer output in terms of pictorial, animated displays, or the behavior of the computer. My distinction betweeen AI and AB is predominately due to AB's emphasis on lifelike representation of the computer model's output.

As an example of a rule for a human emotion, consider the word *frustration*. Many contemporary researchers in psychology define frustration as "Behavior that occurs when there is a negative discrepancy between what occurs in the world and what an individual expects to occur." To put the matter simply, we feel frustrated when we expect 36 inches of snow to fall prior to a winter ski holiday, and now it is February and there hasn't been even a flurry of the white stuff! The rule here is, what occurs (0 inches of snow) minus what we expect (36 inches of snow) is negative $(0 - 36 = -36)$. Thus, the situation frustrates us. Behaviors that result when an individual is frustrated can include aggression, regression, daydreaming, persistence, and repression. The type of behavior a frustrated individual exhibits will vary depending on the circumstances of his or her environment and prior experience. The character in the adventure game we imagined in the opening sentences of this chapter showed his frustration by kicking the closed garage door that he expected to be open.

Chapter 2 will describe how we can simulate facial expression of emotion using a set of rules from the scientific literature. Chapters 3, 4, and 5 will describe the computer simulation of rules about expectations, frustration, and courage. Subsequent chapters will describe how the computer simulation of these rules result in complex emotions and behavior.

Many chapters of this book will present rules for describing one or more psychological states. Then a BASIC program will be presented for interactive, animated graphics simulation of the psychological states. The purpose of this book is to introduce techniques for the development of Artificial Behavior, or humanlike machines.

WHY CREATE ARTIFICIAL BEHAVIOR

There are a wide variety of potential uses for Artificial Behavior techniques. They can be used as subroutines in computer games and robotics. Artificial Behavior programs can be used in educational settings to teach people about psychology. There are potential applications for AB in self-analysis, research, and robotics. I will introduce some applications of AB in the next few paragraphs and then return to this topic on occasion throughout the rest of the book.

In teaching psychology courses in college, I find that my students frequently object to the idea that rules have anything to do with expectations, frustration, hope, or any other human emotions. My students constantly attempt to discourage me from teaching them about rules governing psychological processes. They try to avoid learning rules in my classes by reminding me that logic and mathematics are not prerequisites for my courses. They tell me they are studying psychology because they don't like mathematics and science. The challenge for me has been to make the learning about rules that describe behavior interesting and enjoyable. One technique that I have been using to gain the interest and attention of students (and colleagues, I hasten to add) has been to use the rules I want them to know about in animated graphics computer programs. In these programs, students use the computer keyboard to control the events occurring on the screen display, and these events affect the behavior of the animated graphics characters.

I originally wrote the program RAT RACE (Chapters 3, 4, and 5), for example, to challenge my students to learn rules governing the effects of rewards on behavior. In this program, a hungry rat is placed in the start box of a straight runway. The student must type in the number of food pellets the rat will get in the goal box after scampering down the runway. When the rat is rewarded with food, its running speed increases (it comes to expect the food and behaves appropriately). If the food is withheld following a half dozen or more food-rewarded runs, the rat is frustrated (it doesn't get the food it expects). This program, as you will learn in later chapters, uses a rule that describes such things as expectancy, frustration, courage, persistence, elation, and depression. That an animated organism on the computer screen behaves this way is exciting and interesting to students. Since they know that computers involve math and science, they begin to wonder how it is possible to illustrate emotions in a computer program unless emotions may in fact be formalized in rules. And that, of course, is the point. Some emotions may be described by rules. Artificial Behavior software demonstrates it, and what has often been an unpleasant learning experience becomes an exciting process of discovery.

I also use Artificial Behavior programs as a research tool. These research programs generate predictions about how individuals will behave in situations they have not yet experienced. The predictions are then evaluated by conducting experiments with real people and comparing the results to the predictions. Such a process (represented in Figure 1-1) helps us refine the programs, and at the same time it teaches us a great deal about human behavior. Another application of mine involves clinical psychology interns using AB programs as an aid in designing therapy programs for hypothetical clients who must be diagnosed and treated. Artificial Behavior can be very helpful in answering "what-if" questions about the effects of environmental manipulations on behavior, and it can do so in a cost-effective, safe, and humane way.

Potential applications of AB techniques extend beyond the world of education. Consider, for example, the prospects for more challenging and interesting computer games. Computer adventure games currently use conditional branching techniques to assign psychological traits, such as courage or anger, to their characters. As a result, characters change unrealistically. The traits that they display have been assigned to them by the whimsical notions of the programmer or player. Artificial Behavior will allow behavior changes to take place naturally as a character interacts with his environment. Such changes will be governed by rules that have been developed by experts in the field of human behavior. The behavior of characters in such games will change as a function of their experience. Artificial Behavior adventure games might evolve to the point where a player can introduce new characters into the game and then watch as the characters established in earlier sessions of play adjust to the new cast. Such games would turn out differently each time they were played, and users could find themselves involved in the creation of an interactive fiction filled with lifelike friends and foes, characters who seem to have minds of their own. The goals of AB adventure games might be quite different from the goals of today's standard adventure game. Instead of fighting dragons and gnomes for the sake of winning clues and finding implements, the user might seek character-building experiences.

Artificial Behavior subroutines might even be used to enhance arcade-type computer games. In almost all contemporary computer arcade games, screen characters, such as PacMan, have a very limited repertoire of behavior that remains fairly constant. Using AB, a programmer could make the character's behavior more variable and lifelike.

Foresight and imagination might someday lead to AB computer software that quizzes and challenges a home computer user, or plays a game with him or her, and in the process creates a file that acquires a personality that mirrors the user's own traits. Such a program would be a valuable aid to self-observation and self-knowledge. The user could use the program to predict his or her own behavior, and if desired, he or she could then learn to change it.

Artificial Behavior uses the computer to represent behaving individuals in a changing environment, and so far we have been discussing the simulation of this behavior on the computer screen. We should remember, however, that a computer may display behavior in other ways as well, such as by writing data to a disk or to memory, sending messages to a printer, speaking with the aid of a speech synthesizer, or playing music. And robotics will further extend the behavioral repertoire of electronic devices. AB can be used to create machines that move, lift, touch, bite, kick, and so on in humanlike ways. All that needs to be done is to install the rules describing human behavior as part of the operating system of the computer or robot. Then, if you don't behave the way your computer expects you to, it may kick *you* instead of the garage door. Clearly, AB can be used to incorporate into machines our knowledge about human behavior to create helpmates, friends, teachers, employees, and enemies, as well as our current computer chess opponents and psychotherapists.

Once again, imagine a computer that expresses joy, rage, anger, fear, surprise, and disgust. Imagine a computer that learns from experience, becomes frustrated, and shows courage and persistence. Imagine a computer that is afraid, superstitious, has hopes, is relieved, makes choices, lies, teases, is cooperative, aggressive, helpful, and at other times anxious. Imagine a computer that knows and understands your behavior, one that helps you to understand yourself. Using scientific principles to create Artificial Behavior programs was once thought to be only science fiction, but it is possible now. Those who become proficient in the programming of AB ultimately will create computers that become our best friends, computers that we cannot turn off because we would feel guilty if we did, computers that become mirrors of their users, computers that help us know and change ourselves. But don't just imagine genuinely animated machines; turn the page and start learning how to create one for yourself.

ADDITIONAL READINGS

The following references are provided for readers who are interested in pursuing additional material on topics covered in this chapter.

Artificial Intelligence. These books provide overviews of this field, and are listed from simplest to most complex.

1. Gloess, P. Y., *Understanding Artificial Intelligence* (Sherman Oaks, Calif.: Alfred Publishing, 1981).
2. Winston, P. H., *Artificial Intelligence* (Menlo Park, Calif.: Addison-Wesley, 1979).
3 . Norman, D. A., *Perspectives on Cognitive Science* (Norwood, N.J.: Albex Publishing, 1981).

Applications of Artificial Intelligence. The first book surveys attempts to use AI to develop computer programs that play chess, and the second book describes the development and implementation of a medical diagnosis program.

4. Frey, P. W. (ed.), *Chess Skills in Man and Machines* (New York: Springer-Verlag, 1977).
5. Shortliffe, E. H., *Computer-based Medical Consultations: MYCIN* (New York: Elsevier, 1976).

Artificial Behavior.   The first book presents a very readable version of the approach to psychology that emphasizes behavior. The second book is a textbook with excellent chapters on behaviorism and information processing theories of behavior.

6. Rachlin, H., *Behaviorism in Everyday Life* (Englewood Cliffs, N.J.: Prentice-Hall, Inc., 1980).
7. Bower, G. H., and Hilgard, E. R., *Theories of Learning,* 5th ed. (Englewood Cliffs, N.J.: Prentice-Hall, Inc., 1981).

2

FACIAL EXPRESSION OF EMOTION

Program Faces

Most books, magazine articles, and television programs present the theory of evolution as a description of the historical development of various forms of life. These presentations focus on physical structure. Emphasis is placed on the description, for example, of the development of feathers on birds from scales on fish. The similarity of physical structure of humans and apes, apes and monkeys, and monkeys and other mammals, is considered to be evidence for the idea that all life forms develop from other life forms. However, Charles Darwin, the person most frequently credited with developing the theory of evolution, also was convinced that psychological processes evolved just as surely as physical structure evolved.

The argument for the evolution of physical structures was proposed in 1859 in Darwin's book *Origin of Species*. The argument for the evolution of psychological processes was set forth by Darwin in a series of six books beginning with *The Expression of the Emotions in Man and Animals,* first published in 1862. In this book, Darwin traced the evolution of emotional expression through such species as cats, dogs, monkeys, and man. The last eight chapters describe the facial expressions of eight categories of emotion: suffering and crying; depression; elation; meditation; anger; disgust; surprise; and modesty.

The evidence that Darwin provided for his argument was primarily anecdotal. He presents stories describing facial expressions in animals that he observed, stories that others told him, descriptions of his own children's facial expressions, and anecdotal observations of facial expressions in humans from many parts of the world. One of Darwin's major conclusions was that the facial expression of emotion is identical in all human cultures. This conclusion is compatible with the hypothesis that psychological processes are evolved. Darwin reasoned that since there is only one species of humans, if their facial expression of emotion has evolved, and if humans share a common ancestry, then all members of the human species should produce and recognize similar facial expressions in similar situations.

Systematic research on Darwin's hypothesis about the universality of facial expression of emotion has been undertaken by Paul Ekman of the University of California, San Francisco. For a period now spanning some twenty years, Dr. Ekman has been gathering data on the question "Do members of all groups of humans show similar facial expressions in similar situations?" What Ekman and others have found (see Additional Readings at the end of the chapter) is that there is convincing evidence that human expressions for the following emotions are universal: happiness, anger, disgust, sadness, fear, and surprise. People label these facial expressions with emotion words of the same meaning in Japan, the United States, the Soviet Union, Malaysia, Mexico, and numerous other cultures. Members of tribal cultures in New Guinea, West Iran, and Australia also label these six facial expressions in the same consistent fashion. In addition, people in various cultures show the same facial expressions when watching films depicting emotion-eliciting events. Although many cultural and individual rules govern facial expression, this research suggests that there is a universal set of facial expressions for these six emotions.

In order to conduct this research, it was necessary to develop a system for labeling facial expressions. The procedure, developed over many years by Ekman, is called the Facial Affect Scoring Technique (FAST). Table 2-1 gives some of the rules for placing facial expressions in the six categories of surprise, fear, anger, disgust, sadness, and happiness. Program FACES is an algorithm for generating computer graphics displays of the facial expressions of emotions. These graphics were developed from the information in Table 2-1.

Each emotion requires rules about eyes and eyelids, eyebrows and forehead, and the mouth and lower face. For each set of rules that define an emotion, a set of subroutines is called that draws the emotional expression. The subroutine for each expression calls drawing routines for various facial characteristics: eyelids, eyes, eyebrows, lips, and so on. For example, a mouth is

TABLE 2-1

	Eyes– Lids	Brows– Forehead	Lower Face
Surprise	wide open eyes	raised, curved brows, long horizontal forehead wrinkles	open mouth
Fear	eyes open hard stare	raised, drawn together brow vertical forehead wrinkles	mouth corners drawn back
Anger	appear squinting	brows together vertical forehead wrinkles	square mouth
Disgust	lower eyelids up and raised	brows down but not together	raised cheeks upper lips raised
Sadness	drooping lids tears	brows together	mouth corners down
Happiness	relaxed narrow eyes	no distinctive appearance	corners of lips raised, cheeks up

(Summarized from Ekman, P., 1972, pp. 251–52.)

defined as consisting of six horizontal parts, three for the upper lip and three for
the lower lip. Surprise is an open-mouthed expression and therefore calls only
the subroutines for the top part of the upper lip and the bottom part of the lower
lip. Each emotional expression is defined as a subset of a larger set of graphics
routines for drawing facial features. And as our knowledge of facial expression
becomes more informed by knowledge of facial muscles, programs such as
FACES can begin to simulate actual muscle contraction and relaxation.

   Program FACES was developed in three steps. First, the descriptions in
Table 2-1 were simplified. Second, a set of drawing routines for parts of facial
features (eyes, mouth, eyebrows, and forehead wrinkles) was written. Third, a
set of subroutines was written that call the appropriate set of drawing routines
for each of the six facial expressions. FACES almost instantly produces graphic
illustrations of the six facial expressions. Instead of having six full drawings, a
set of parts of features is programmed that can then be used to produce all six
expressions. The algorithmic nature of FACES makes it possible to generate

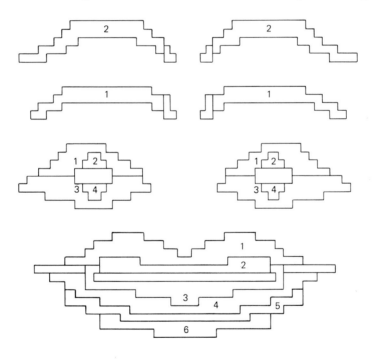

Figure 2-1.   Graphics of facial features parts used in program FACES. The top row
shows eyebrows that are arched and elongated. Second row is eyebrows that are
straight and slightly shorter. The third row is a pair of eyes and the four parts that are
used to depict wide open (light 1 and 3) or partly closed (light 1, 2, 3, and 4) eyes. The
bottom is a pair of lips that can be completely closed or open to various degrees. The
numbers correspond to the entries in Table 2-2. These graphics parts and Table 2-2
constitute an algorithm used to show the six facial expressions of emotion in program
FACES.

additional expressions by calling combinations of parts other than those that define the six basic emotions. We will return to this characteristic of program FACES when we discuss its applications.

Reading down the third column of Table 2-1 suggests that one important way in which these six expressions differ is the extent to which the mouth is open or closed. On the basis of this difference in the six expressions, a mouth was drawn as shown in Figure 2-1. The mouth is subdivided into six parts, as indicated in the drawing. Each part of the mouth is programmed as a separate subroutine. Surprise has a wide-open mouth and calls mouth parts 1, 2, 5, and 6. Anger has pressed lips and calls mouth parts 1, 2, 3, 4, 5, and 6. Fear is indicated with a long, narrow, closed mouth and calls parts 1, 2, 3, and 4. Disgust is indicated by having the upper lip raised and calls parts 1, 3, and 4. Sadness calls parts 1, 2, 4, and 5, and happiness calls parts 1, 2, 4, and 5.

A similar approach was used to define eye parts, two types of eyebrows, and three types of forehead wrinkles. Figure 2-1 shows the mouth and its parts, the eyes and their parts, and the two types of eyebrows. Table 2-2 indicates which parts of each feature are used by the program FACES to draw each of the six facial expressions of emotion. Figure 2-1 and Table 2-2 constitute the algorithm used by the program FACES to generate six sets of facial features corresponding to six facial expressions of emotion. Figure 2-2 illustrates the six computer generated facial expressions produced by the program FACES on your computer monitor.

TABLE 2-2

Emotion	Eyes	Brows	Mouth	Forehead Wrinkles	Other
Surprise	1, 4	2	1, 2, 5, 6	long horizontal	
Fear	1, 4	2	1, 2, 3, 4	short vertical	brows together
Anger	1, 2, 3, 4	1	1, 2, 3, 4 5, 6	vertical	brows together square mouth
Disgust	1, 3, 4	1	1, 3, 4	—	straight cheeks
Sadness	1, 2, 4	1	1, 2, 4, 5	short horizontal	tears
Happiness	1, 2, 4	1	1, 2, 3, 4	—	cheeks and mouth raised

The descriptions of facial features given in Table 2-1 define characteristics of six emotional expressions. The facial features drawn in Figure 2-2 have been given numbers to represent their various parts. The entries in this table specify which facial features parts (using the numbered parts from Figure 2-1) must be dispayed for the computer to generate a drawing of a face that shows each of the six emotional expressions.

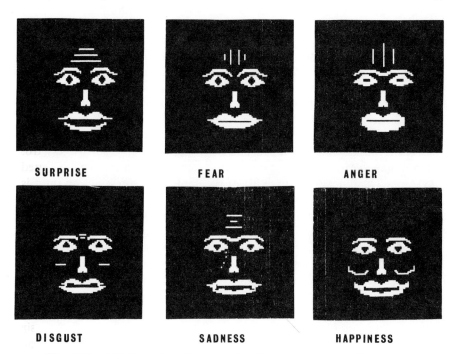

Figure 2-2. This figure shows the six emotional expressions generated by program FACES. These illustrations are dumps to a dot matrix printer of high-resolution screen displays.

DESCRIPTION OF PROGRAM FACES

Program FACES is written as a guessing game. The computer generates faces and the user guesses the expression from the list of six emotions. The computer then indicates whether your guess was correct or incorrect and displays your accumulated percentage of correct guesses.

Lines 100 through 180 print brief instructions on the screen and wait for the user to hit any key to begin. The variable A$ at line 180 is the input variable for any key press to begin executing the remainder of the program. Line 190 sets the variable C equal to 0. The variable C counts the number of faces the computer generates. This value will be used at line 420 to calculate the percent of correct guesses. Line 200 increments C by 1. This is the line that the program will return to before it generates another face.

Line 210 calls a subroutine at line 720. The subroutine located at lines 720 through 760 draws a nose on the screen and returns control to line 220. Line 220 increments the variable X by 1. The variable X is used in line 230 to subscript the RND function when generating a random number. The function RND must have a new subscript each time it is called or it will produce the same random number over and over again. Lines 240 and 250 direct the machine to generate a new random number if the one it has generated is smaller than 0 or larger than 6. The program has now generated a random number (assigned to the variable Y), with a range of 1 to 6. If the random number Y is equal to 1, line 260 assigns the letter S, for surprise, to the variable Y$, and sends control to the subroutine for surprise located at line 500. If Y = 2, line 270 sets Y$ equal to F, for fear, and calls the subroutine for fear at line 530. Similarly, if Y = 3, Y$ = A for anger and the subroutine for anger is called. Y = 4 is disgust, Y = 5 is sadness, and Y = 6 is happiness.

Lines 320 and 340 print the list of six emotional expressions on the text window at the bottom of the screen. Line 340 accepts the user's guess (B$) and lines 350 through 380 evaluate it by comparing it to Y$, and then printing out "correct" or "incorrect". Lines 390 through 430 calculate the percent of correct guesses and print it to the text area of the screen. Lines 440 through 480 ask the user whether he wants the computer to generate another face and branch back to line 200 if he does, or clear the screen and end if he doesn't. The remainder of the program lines (490–1370) are subroutines containing the features drawing algorithm. These subroutines are described by the REMarks before each section of BASIC code.

PROGRAM LISTING

```
0100    CLEAR:HOME:PRINT:PRINT:PRINT
0110    PRINT "THE COMPUTER WILL DRAW A FACE.":PRINT
0120    PRINT "IT WILL THEN NAME SIX EMOTIONS.":PRINT
0130    PRINT "GUESS THE EMOTION BY TYPING IN THE "
0140    PRINT "LETTER INDICATED ON THE SCREEN.":PRINT
0150    PRINT "THE COMPUTER WILL THEN TELL YOU IF YOU"
0160    PRINT "ARE RIGHT OR WRONG. PRESS ANY KEY
        TO BEGIN.":PRINT:PRINT
0170    PRINT:PRINT:PRINT:PRINT:PRINT
0180    GET A$
0190    C=0
0200    C=C+1
0210    GOSUB 720
0220    X=X+1
0230    Y=INT(10*RND(X))
0240    IF Y<1 THEN GOTO 220
0250    IF Y>6 THEN GOTO 220
0260    IF Y=1 THEN Y$="S":GOSUB 500
0270    IF Y=2 THEN Y$="F":GOSUB 530
0280    IF Y=3 THEN Y$="A":GOSUB 560
0290    IF Y=4 THEN Y$="D":GOSUB 610
0300    IF Y=5 THEN Y$="N":GOSUB 640
0310    IF Y=6 THEN Y$="H":GOSUB 690
0320    PRINT "SURPRISE(S)      FEAR(F)        ANGER(A) "
0330    PRINT "DISGUST(D)       SADNESS(N)     HAPPINESS(H) "
```

```
0340    INPUT B$
0350    IF B$=Y$ THEN GOTO 370
0360    GOTO 380
0370    PRINT "CORRECT":GOTO 390
0380    PRINT "INCORRECT"
0390    IF B$=Y$ THEN GOTO 410
0400    GOTO 420
0410    B=B+1
0420    D=INT (100*(B/C))
0430    PRINT "YOU HAVE "B" CORRECT OF "C" FACES, "D"%"
0440    PRINT "ANOTHER FACE? (Y/N)"
0450    INPUT F$
0460    IF F$="Y" THEN GOTO 200
0470    GOTO 480
0480    TEXT:HOME:END
0490    REM    ********************
0500    REM    SURPRISE SUBROUTINE
0510    GOSUB 840:GOSUB 950:GOSUB 1040:GOSUB 1230:GOSUB 1260:
        GOSUB 1330:GOSUB 1360:RETURN
0520    REM    ********************
0530    REM    FEAR SUBROUTINE
0540    GOSUB 800:GOSUB 950:GOSUB 980:GOSUB 1040:GOSUB 1230:
        GOSUB 1260:GOSUB 1280:GOSUB 1300:RETURN
0550    REM    ********************
0560    REM    ANGER SUBROUTINE
0570    GOSUB 820:GOSUB 920:GOSUB 1000:GOSUB 1040:GOSUB 1100:
        GOSUB 1120:GOSUB 1230:GOSUB 1260:
        GOSUB 1280:GOSUB 1300:GOSUB 1330:GOSUB 1360
0580    HCOLOR=0:HPLOT 122,108 TO 126,108 TO 126,109 TO 125,109:
        HPLOT 167,108 TO 163,108 TO 163,109 TO 164,109
0590    HCOLOR=3:HPLOT 142,77 TO 148,77 TO 148,78 TO 142,78:
        RETURN
0600    REM    ********************
0610    REM    DISGUST SUBROUTINE
0620    GOSUB 880:GOSUB 920:GOSUB 1040:GOSUB 1120:GOSUB 1230:
        GOSUB 1280:GOSUB 1300:GOSUB 1160:RETURN
0630    REM    ********************
0640    REM    SADNESS SUBROUTINE
0650    GOSUB 860:GOSUB 920:GOSUB 1000:GOSUB 1040:GOSUB 1100:
        GOSUB 1230:GOSUB 1260:GOSUB 1300:GOSUB 1330
0660    HPLOT 142,77 TO 148,77 TO 148,78 TO 142,78:HPLOT
        138,86:HPLOT 138,89:HPLOT 136,93:HPLOT 134,96
0670    HCOLOR=0:HPLOT 134,104 TO 138,104:HPLOT 151,104 TO
        156,104:HPLOT 129,111 TO 131,111:HPLOT 158,111 TO
        161,111:HCOLOR=3:HPLOT 131,108 TO 132,108:HPLOT
        158,108 TO 159,108:RETURN
0680    REM    ********************
0690    REM    HAPPINESS SUBROUTINE
0700    GOSUB 920:GOSUB 1040:GOSUB 1100:GOSUB 1230:GOSUB 1260:
        GOSUB 1300:GOSUB 1330:GOSUB 1180
0710    HPLOT 122,107 TO 126,107:HPLOT 163,107 TO 167,107:
        :HPLOT 124,106 TO 122,106 TO 122,
        105:HPLOT 165,106 TO 167,106 TO 167,105:RETURN
0720    REM    DRAWS NOSE
0730    POKE 230,32:CALL 62450:HGR:HCOLOR=3
```

```
0740    HPLOT 148,99 TO 148,97:HPLOT 147,96 TO 147,99 TO
        146,99 TO 146,89 TO 145,89 TO 144,99 TO 144,89 TO
        143,89 TO 143,99 TO 142,99 TO 142,96:HPLOT 141,97
        TO 141,99
0750    HCOLOR=3

0760    RETURN
0770    REM   ********************
0780    REM   FOREHEAD SUBROUTINES
0790    REM   FEAR
0800    HPLOT 136,64 TO 136,67:HPLOT 141,61 TO 141,70:HPLOT
        148,61 TO 148,70:HPLOT 153,64 TO 153,67:RETURN
0810    REM   ANGER
0820    HPLOT 136,70 TO 136,61:HPLOT 145,72 TO 145,57:HPLOT
        153,70 TO 153,61:RETURN
0830    REM   SURPRISE
0840    HPLOT 139,61 TO 151,61:HPLOT 135,65 TO 154,65:HPLOT
        132,69 TO 157,69:RETURN
0850    REM   SADNESS
0860    HPLOT 139,61 TO 151,61:HPLOT 142,65 TO 147,65:HPLOT
        138,69 TO 151,69:RETURN
0870    REM   DISGUST
0880    HPLOT 142,74 TO 147,74:HPLOT 143,76 TO 146,76:RETURN
0890    REM   ********************
0900    REM   EYEBROW SUBROUTINES
0910    REM   BROWS 1
0920    HPLOT 120,78 TO 121,78 TO 121,77 TO 124,77 TO 124,76
        TO 140,76 TO 140,77 TO 139,77:HPLOT 125,75 TO 138,75
0930    HPLOT 169,78 TO 168,78 TO 168,77 TO 166,77 TO
        166,76 TO 149,76 TO 149,77 TO 150,77:HPLOT 151,75 TO
        164,75:RETURN
0940    REM   BROWS 2
0950    HPLOT 118,78 TO 121,78 TO 121,77 TO 124,77 TO 124,76
        TO 126,76:HPLOT 125,75 TO 138,75:HPLOT 126,74 TO 137,
        74:HPLOT 137,76 TO 140,76 TO 140,77
0960    HPLOT 171,78 TO 168,78 TO 168,77 TO 165,77 TO 165,76 TO
        163,76:HPLOT 164,75 TO 151,75:HPLOT 163,74 TO 152,74:
        HPLOT 152,76 TO 149,76 TO 149,77:RETURN
0970    REM   BROWS 3
0980    HPLOT 141,77 TO 141,78 TO 142,78:HPLOT 148,77 TO
        148,78 TO 147,78:RETURN
0990    REM   BROWS 4
1000    HPLOT 141,76 TO 141,78 TO 142,78:HPLOT 148,76 TO
        148,78 TO 147,78:RETURN
1010    REM   ********************
1020    REM   EYE SUBROUTINES
1030    REM   EYES 1 AND 4
1040    HPLOT 127,78 TO 132,78:HPLOT 157,78 TO 162,78:HPLOT
        126,79 TO 129,79:HPLOT 132,79 TO 134,79:HPLOT 155,79 TO
        157,79:HPLOT 160,79 TO 163,79
1050    HPLOT 125,80 TO 128,80:HPLOT 133,80 TO 136,80:HPLOT
        153,80 TO 156,80:HPLOT 161,80 TO 164,80:HPLOT 123,81
        TO 127,81:HPLOT 134,81 TO
        138,81:HPLOT 151,81 TO 155,81:HPLOT 162,81 TO 166,81
1060    HPLOT 121,82 TO 127,82:HPLOT 134,82 TO 139,82:HPLOT
```

```
         150,82 TO 155,82:HPLOT 162,82 TO 168,82:HPLOT 120,83 TO
         TO 128,83:HPLOT 133,83 TO 139,83:HPLOT 150,83 TO 156,83:
         HPLOT 161,83 TO 169,83
1070     HPLOT 124,84 TO 129,84:HPLOT 132,84 TO 136,84:HPLOT
         153,84 TO 157,84:HPLOT 160,84 TO 165,84:HPLOT 128,85
         TO 133,85:HPLOT 156,85 TO 161,85
1080     RETURN
1090     REM   EYES 2
1100     HPLOT 130,79 TO 131,79:HPLOT 129,80 TO 132,80:HPLOT
         158,79 TO 159,79:HPLOT 157,80 TO 160,80:RETURN
1110     REM   EYES 3
1120     HPLOT 130,84 TO 131,84:HPLOT 129,83 TO 132,83:HPLOT
         158,84 TO 159,84:HPLOT 157,83 TO 160,83:RETURN
1130     REM   ********************
1140     REM   CHEEKS SUBROUTINE
1150     REM   DISGUST
1160     HPLOT 122,94 TO 130,94:HPLOT 159,94 TO 167,94:RETURN
1170     REM   HAPPINESS
1180     HPLOT 117,94 TO 117,97 TO 120,97 TO 120,98 TO 122,98
         TO 122,99 TO 131,99 TO 131,98 TO 132,98 TO
 132,97 TO 133,97
1190     HPLOT 172,94 TO 172,97 TO 169,97 TO 169,98 TO 167,98 TO
         167,99 TO 158,99 TO 158,98 TO 157,98 TO 157,97 TO
         156,97:RETURN
1200     REM   ********************
1210     REM   MOUTH SUBROUTINES
1220     REM   LIPS 1
1230     HPLOT 134,104 TO 138,104:HPLOT 151,104 TO 156,104:HPLOT
         131,105 TO 141,105:HPLOT 148,105 TO 158,105:HPLOT 130,106
         TO 143,106
1240     HPLOT 146,106 TO 159,106:HPLOT 127,107 TO 131,107:HPLOT
         138,107 TO 151,107:HPLOT 158,107 TO 162,107:RETURN
1250     REM   LIPS 2
1260     HPLOT 132,107 TO 137,107:HPLOT 152,107 TO 157,107:
         HPLOT 122,108 TO 129,108:HPLOT 132,108 TO 157,108:
         HPLOT 160,108 TO 167,108:RETURN
1270     REM   LIPS 3
1280     HPLOT 131,108 TO 130,108 TO 130,110 TO 159,110 TO 159,
         108 TO 158,108:HPLOT 137,111 TO 152,111:HPLOT 143,112
         TO 146,112:RETURN
1290     REM   LIPS 4
1300     HPLOT 125,109 TO 129,109:HPLOT 160,109 TO 164,109:
         HPLOT 127,110 TO 129,110:HPLOT 160,110 TO 162,110:HPLOT
         129,111 TO 136,111
1310     HPLOT 153,111 TO 160,111:HPLOT 132,112 TO 142,112:
         HPLOT 147,112 TO 157,112:HPLOT 136,113 TO 153,113:RETURN
1320     REM   LIPS 5
1330     HPLOT 127,111 TO 128,111:HPLOT 161,111 TO 162,111:
         HPLOT 127,112 TO 131,112:HPLOT 158,112 TO 162,112
1340     HPLOT 130,113 TO 135,113:HPLOT 154,113 TO 159,113:HPLOT
         135,114 TO 154,114:RETURN
1350     REM   LIPS 6
1360     HPLOT 132,114 TO 134,114:HPLOT 155,114 TO 157,114:
         HPLOT 132,115 TO 157,115:HPLOT 140,116 TO 149,116:RETURN
1370     REM   ********************
```

After you have typed in the program, proofread it, and save it to a disk or cassette tape. Now you may simply RUN the program. As indicated earlier, the program will randomly select an emotion and draw the facial features on the screen. You will be asked to type in a guess of the emotion using the six names for the emotions and the corresponding letters displayed on the bottom of the screen. The program will then tell you if the guess is correct or incorrect. It also will print out the number of faces that have been displayed, the number of correct guesses, and the percentage of correct guesses. The program then will ask you whether or not you want to see another face.

Notice that facial expressions of emotion generated by this program are not of the same exaggerated type produced by other "face-making" software. In those programs, entirely different sets of eyes, mouths, and other facial parts can be combined to make happy or sad faces. Although the present technique produces faces that differ from one another in very subtle ways, they are realistic. Each of the facial characteristics, such as eyes and mouth always have the same basic dimensions. As depicted in Figure 2-1, the full features were broken into constituent parts that were then combined in various ways to illustrate a variety of emotions. This approach produces a more accurate simulation of the changes in facial expression of a single person.

APPLICATIONS IN DAILY LIFE

Program FACES was developed to illustrate the use of a formal scheme for categorizing observational data in psychological research. A college student can practice the rules in Table 2-1 by using the program FACES. Then the student is more likely to classify correctly the expressions of humans when making research observations of facial expression of emotion.

Children enjoy playing with this program. Six and seven year olds guess correctly with only a small amount of practice. Even younger children can use it as an adjunct to learning the words we use to label feelings. The real world offers only limited opportunities for children to learn how other people feel. Playing with the program FACES will augment that experience. A child who becomes adept at discriminating the subtle differences in emotional expression produced by the computer will have increased opportunities to learn to be sensitive to other people's feelings. This program is an excellent teaching tool to assist children in learning to discriminate facial expression of emotion.

Many adults have never learned to judge correctly the facial expressions of other people. These individuals often have difficulties in their day-to-day interactions with friends, co-workers, and family members. Since they do not know that their friend is angry, for example, they say or do something that makes their friend even more angry. This type of situation can lead to verbal and physical aggression. Most psychotherapists can describe a client who had day-to-day difficulties in living that were reduced when the client learned to be more sensitive to other people's feelings. Program FACES can help many such individuals learn to discriminate the facial expressions of emotion in other people.

Psychologists know that people communicate with facial expressions and body language, as well as with verbal behavior. When we ask our co-worker, for example, "How's your mother doing?", we may learn more by watching the facial expression of the person than we learn by listening to what they say. Facial expressions of emotion, like so many facets of daily life, are something that we typically learn about in a haphazard manner. Program FACES can help most people learn useful skills to help them recognize the emotional state of others. We also must keep in mind, however, that control of facial expression can be learned. It is not necessarily the case that facial expressions are the road to someone's feelings. Many people have learned to always look happy or to always look sad. In these cases, we need to listen to what they say, *and* watch what they do, before we make inferences about how they feel. Increased skill at reading faces also can help us detect consistencies and inconsistencies in other people's expressions.

APPLICATIONS TO RESEARCH

Paul Ekman has hypothesized that the expression of many additional human emotions may be produced by other combinations of the facial features parts identified in Figure 2-1 and Table 2-2. Program FACES could be easily modified to produce all possible combinations of features parts contained in its subroutines. The expressions produced in this way could be shown to a sample of people in a culture with the request that they try to assign an emotional expression label (word) to the face. A smirk, for example, may combine some of the facial features parts of happiness and anger. A grimace may combine features of anger and disgust (in fact, this is similar to Darwin's hypothesis regarding the evolution of the grimace expression). A grin might combine some features of a smile and anger. The number of possible combinations is quite large. Ekman's hypothesis could be tested using facial expressions generated by the algorithm contained in the program FACES.

APPLICATIONS TO OTHER COMPUTER SOFTWARE

Program FACES, or the algorithm on which it is based, has uses in other types of computer software. Its use of an algorithm containing parts of facial features allows for a small, compact program that can rapidly generate facial expressions of emotion. These characteristics make it an ideal candidate for incorporation into other software. Instructional programs, for example, frequently provide feedback on the correctness or incorrectness of a student's responses by printing out words like "correct" or "incorrect" on the screen. School teachers have found that human facial expressions provide more effective feedback and place stickers of happy faces or sad faces on students' papers to indicate their approval or disapproval of a student's work. The algorithm on which FACES is based could be used to generate facial expression in one corner of the screen of an instructional program. The expression on the face would provide feedback to the user as he or she solved the problems the program presented, or made mistakes. The student's progress in the lessons would serve to keep the "instructor" looking happy. And the student's errors would generate expressions of disapproval or sadness. The task for the student would not only be the act of progressing through the program but the challenge of keeping the computer happy. This feedback would enhance the student's attention to the task and performance.

The algorithm also could be used in computer games. The ghostlike characters in PacMan games could change their expressions to fear when they were under attack by PacMan. They could look surprised when PacMan came around the corner. Sets of facial features designed around the algorithm in FACES could be used in all types of gaming software (arcade games, adventure games, educational games, etc.) to generate facial expressions that indicate the emotion most appropriate to the current gaming situation. Since six of the facial expressions can be interpreted independent of culture, the games using this technique may acquire broader international markets by incorporating this technique.

SUMMARY

In the nineteenth century, Charles Darwin offered the hypothesis that psychological processes were evolved as surely as anatomical and physiological processes. His early work involved the study of the evolution of facial expression of emotion. Subsequent research, spearheaded by Paul Ekman, has found that the facial expression of surprise, fear, anger, disgust, sadness, and happiness are universally recognized in the human species. Ekman's Facial Affect Scoring Technique yielded descriptions of the facial features unique to these six emotions. These descriptions were used to develop an algorithm, based on parts of facial features (eyes, mouth, brows, and forehead wrinkles), which can be used to rapidly generate graphics displays of facial expression of emotion. Program FACES is presented as an example of computer simulation of a facial expression of emotion algorithm. This program can be used to teach children and adults how to recognize the facial expression of emotion of other people. The technique used in program FACES can be used to provide graphics feedback in instructional programs, to generate new expressions of emotion and test their correspondence to real world human expression, and can be incorporated into computer games to create more lifelike characters.

ADDITIONAL READINGS

Evolution of Emotional Expression.   Due to the continuing value of Darwin's research and analysis, his book has been reprinted. It provides an excellent overview of the argument for evolution of emotional expression in humans.

1. Darwin, C. *The Expression of the Emotions in Man and Animals.* Chicago: The University of Chicago Press, 1965 (originally published in 1862).

Facial Expression of Emotion.   The following two papers provide excellent overviews of the development of the Facial Affect Scoring Technique and current research supporting the argument of universality of facial expression and recognition of emotion.

2. Ekman, P. "Universals and Cultural Differences in Facial Expressions of Emotion," in J. K. Cole (ed.), *Nebraska Symposium on Motivation,* Vol. XIX (Lincoln: University of Nebraska Press, 1972), pp. 207–83.
3. Ekman, P., and Oster, H., "Facial Expressions of Emotion," in M. R. Rosenzweig and L. W. Porter (eds.) *Annual Review of Psychology,* Vol. 30 (Palo Alto, Calif.: Annual Reviews Inc., 1979), pp. 527–54.

3

EXPECTATIONS OF REWARDS

Program
RAT RACE 1

In Chapter 1, we imagined a computer that came to expect certain kinds of behavior from its user and was frustrated when those expectations were not met. The creation of a computer program that simulates the development of expectations and frustration begins in this chapter with a discussion of RAT RACE, a program to illustrate the relationship between reward and behavior. RAT RACE 1 will simulate the development of expectations, RAT RACE 2 will add the development of frustration, and RAT RACE 3 the development of courage.

The model of expectations developed in this chapter provides a foundation in subsequent chapters for the simulation of depression, resistance to change, spontaneity, choice, and superstition. By the time the model is fully developed in Chapter 8, it will simulate a large number of complex psychological phenomena.

This chapter presents a rule for the development of expectations. This rule for changes in expectations is essential for programs presented later in this book.

EXPECTATIONS

In this section, you will discover that several rules must be combined to develop a model of expectations. The first rule is that the behaviors that are followed by reward increase in strength and frequency. For example, if the first time a person puts two quarters into a vending machine he gets back a candy bar, he is going to be more likely to put two quarters into the machine the next time he gets a craving for sweets. If a hungry rat is given food at the end of a runway, he will run faster the next time he is placed there. Many psychologists think of this change in behavior as indicative of a change in expectations. The person's behavior suggests that they expect the candy machine to dispense candy bars in exchange for quarters. The hungry rat behaves as if he expects the goal area of the runway to contain food after he runs the runway. The simple example of learning about the candy machine, or learning about the runway, becomes more intriguing, however, when we notice that candy bars or food pellets don't always change behavior or expectations.

Although rewards can alter expectations, psychologists have observed that they don't always do so. Once a person has learned that his behavior will be followed by a reward, the reward no longer changes his behavior very much. When a rat learns from many experiences to expect food at the end of a runway, additional rewarding experiences do not increase the rat's running speed. When a person learns to expect candy from a vending machine, his eagerness to put money in the machine is not increased by further successful transactions with the machine. The second rule is that rewards are not very effective when they are not surprising. Another way to state this rule is to say that rewards are most effective in changing behavior when they are the most surprising (or least expected). The greater the difference between expectations and reward, the greater the change in our behavior.

We now have two rules about the development of expectations. First, rewards produce increases in expectations. Second, the amount of change in an expectation is a function of how surprising the reward is. It is easy to write an equation for the development of expectations that contains both of these rules.

Symbolizing obtained reward with the letter O, and the expectation of reward with $E+$, we calculate the difference between obtained reward and expectations as $O - E+$. The quantity obtained reward minus expected reward $(O - E+)$ captures our intuitive notion of surprise. If a person obtains a large unexpected reward $(O - E+$ is large), he is surprised. If a person obtains just the reward that he expects $(O - E+$ is 0), he is not surprised. Thus, when $O - E+$ is large, the person is surprised; when it is small, he is not surprised. The amount of change in expectations depends on how surprising the rewards are, the quantity $O - E+$ will be part of the model for describing the development of expectations.

To see how the quantity $O - E+$ actually helps describe changes in expectations, consider the following example. If a person has never used a vending machine and expects nothing from one, we would say that his or her expectations are low. We might assign the value 5 to $E+$. When this person puts two quarters in the machine, he or she is surprised when a chocolate bar is received in return. Assuming 100 to represent the value of an obtained chocolate bar, $O - E+ = 100 - 5 = 95$. The difference between obtained and expected reward is large. Reward in this case is surprising, and there will be a large change in the person's expectations. Someone more accustomed to vending machines would have a higher degree of expectation. Assigning the value 98 to this second person's expectation, and maintaining the value of the chocolate bar at 100, we can see that the difference between this person's expectation and the reward is low: $100 - 98 = 2$. In this case, the reward is not surprising, and expectations will be changed hardly at all.

The first part of our model for the development of expectations is the fact that rewards only change expectations when they are surprising. The difference between obtained and expected reward $(O - E+)$ captures the fact that only surprising rewards change expectations and behavior.

To make the equation complete, we must incorporate two more rules about experience with rewards. First, we must consider the value of the reward itself. When the vending machine gives a person a chocolate bar, the value of the reward might be 100; but if it dispenses a jellybean, the value of the reward may be diminished to a value of 10. For most people, a chocolate bar is more rewarding than a jellybean. The value of the reward, it is important to observe, will set a limit on the value of a learned expectation. In general, our third rule states that larger rewards produce correspondingly larger values of O in our equation.

The equation also must recognize the fact that expectations are not learned all at once. The development of expectations, psychologists have found, occurs as a result of repeated or numerous experiences. Our fourth rule is that the result of a single rewarding experience is to increase an expectation by a fraction of the difference between obtained and expected reward. We can represent the fraction with the letter F, and when we multiply F times the quantity $O - E+$, we will have a number that indicates the amount of increase in expectation produced by one instance of reward. Expectation is increased by the amount $F(O - E+)$. If a person puts two quarters in a candy machine and receives a chocolate bar, his expectation of receiving a chocolate bar the next time is changed by the amount $F(O - E+)$. We can now write the complete equation for the development of expectations:

$$\Delta E+ \ = \ F(O - E+)$$

where

Δ is the Greek letter delta and represents changes.

$E+$ is the expectation of reward.

F is a constant fraction representing the rate of learning.

O is the value of the obtained reward; the value of O sets the maximum value for learned expectation.

The equation says: "Changes in expectation are equal to a fraction of the difference between the obtained reward and the expected reward." Operation of the equation can be illustrated by using the hypothetical example of a person learning to expect chocolate from a vending machine. For the sake of example, we assume the value of the chocolate is 100 ($O = 100$), and the fraction representing the rate of learning is 0.10 ($F = 0.10$). We also will assume that the person has no previous experience with a vending machine, and his degree of expectancy is 0 ($E+ = 0$).

After putting two quarters in the vending machine and receiving a chocolate bar the first time, the person's expectation of receiving a chocolate bar the next time he uses the machine has risen from 0 to 10. Remember, the obtained reward was 100, the expectancy level before the first trial was 0, and the fraction for the rate of learning was 0.10.

$$\Delta E+ \ = \ F(O - E+)$$
$$\Delta E+ \ = \ 0.1(100 - 0)$$
$$\Delta E+ \ = \ 10$$
$$E+ \ = \ 10$$

The second time the person deposits money in the machine, the fractions and the value of the chocolate bar will be the same but the level of the person's expectation will be 10.

$$\Delta E+ \ = \ 0.1(100 \ - \ 10)$$

$$\Delta E+ \ = \ 9$$

$$E+ \ = \ 10 \ + \ 9 \ = \ 19$$

We call each experience with the candy machine a trial. Prior to the first trial, the person's expectancy was 0. At the end of the first trial, it had risen to 10, and now after the second trial it is incremented nine more units and totals 19.

On each subsequent trial, notice that the change in expectation level becomes smaller and smaller.

$$\Delta E+ \ = \ 0.1(100 \ - \ 19)$$

$$\Delta E+ \ = \ 8$$

$$E+ \ = \ 19 \ + \ 8 \ = \ 27$$

The decreasing amount of learning on each trial is called a learning curve by psychologists. A learning curve illustrates the fact that as an individual comes to expect reward his behavior changes less and less on each successive trial.

The equation $\Delta E+ \ = \ F(O \ - \ E+)$ is fundamental for understanding the relationship between behavior and its consequences. It provides a useful model to simulate the development of expectations, frustration, and courage. Once those simulations are developed, they will begin showing interesting combinations of the three psychological states.

BEHAVIORAL PHENOMENA SIMULATED BY RAT RACE 1

Program RAT RACE is an animated graphics simulation of a common laboratory procedure for studying the effects of reward on behavior. Just as physicists use simple models, like a ball rolling down an inclined plane, to study such things as gravity and momentum, psychologists use simple laboratory models to answer questions about the relationship between behavior and its consequences. One of the most common simplified models used by psychologists is a hungry rat running a straight runway for food reward. In their research, psychologists manipulate the amount or schedule of reward, and measure the running speed of the rats. Program RAT RACE simulates this laboratory procedure by:

1. Displaying two rats in the start boxes of two separate runways
2. Having the program user dispense food pellets into the goal boxes of the runways

3. Having rats then run down the alley to the goal box
4. Calculating the effects of the food pellets on the rats' expectations
5. Accumulating the effects of the current reward and past rewards
6. Using the effects of accumulated experience with food reward (the rats' expectations) to determine the running speed (animation rate) on the next trial

Version 1 of program RAT RACE simulates the learning of expectations about food by the rats, and the effects of those expectations on running speed. The program user can simulate the learning of an expectation by repeatedly rewarding the rat with the same number of food pellets and observing the increases in the rat's running speed. The program user can examine the effects of different reward amounts by giving the two rats different amounts of food. Rats given twenty food pellets will learn to run faster than those given five food pellets per trial.

DESCRIPTION OF PROGRAM RAT RACE 1

Initial Graphics

Execution of the program begins at line 0100 by clearing all variables, clearing the high resolution graphics screen, and calling the graphics mode. Line 0120 sets the graphics color to white. Line 0150 calls a subroutine at lines 0500 through 0700 that draws two runways on the screen. Program control is then returned to line 0160. Line 0160 calls a subroutine at lines 0800 through 0880 that draws in doors blocking the start and goal boxes. This is a separate subroutine because the doors must later be opened to allow the rats to leave the start boxes and run to the goal boxes. Line 0170 calls a subroutine at lines 1000 through 1180 that draws the rats in the start boxes. This is a separate subroutine from the one used for running the alley. When confined in the start box, the rat must curl his tail to fit. When running the runway the rat leaves his tail trailing directly behind him. Line 0180 calls a subroutine at lines 1300 through 1460 that asks the user to specify the number of food pellets each rat will receive upon reaching the goal box.

Input Variables

The input routine in lines 1300 through 1480 contains a two repetition FOR/NEXT loop. When the value of the loop variable (B) is 1, the user is asked to input the number of food pellets rat 1 will receive at the end of the runway. When B is 2, the user is asked to input the number of food pellets for rat 2. The possible values for the number of food pellets ranges from 1 to 20. The input values (number of food pellets) are assigned to the variables R(1) and R(2), respectively. These variables are then used as values of obtained reward in the formula used to calculate changes in expectancies and animation rate in the program.

Program Variables

After the user types in the number of food pellets for each rat, program control returns to line 0200. At this point, pressing any key will begin to execute the animated graphics display. First, the graphics color is set to black (0), and the runway door subroutine (line 0800) is called. This removes the doors from the runways. Next, the subroutine at lines 1000 through 1180 is called. This erases the rats from the start boxes of the runways. The graphics color is then returned to white (3) at line 0240, and line 0250 calls the animation subroutine at line 1600.

Animation Algorithm

The animation subroutine contains the animation algorithm and calls the subroutines that produce the actual animation process in which the rats run from the start box to the goal box. Line 1620 sets two variables, X and Y, to the value of 63. These two variables will be used to specify the location of the rats on the screen. This subroutine then calls another subroutine at lines 2200 through 2350. This subroutine draws in the rats at the coordinates specified in the program lines. This drawing will produce rats outside of the start box with tails extended behind them. Program control is then returned to line 1660 of the animation subroutine.

The animation algorithm is based on the difference between the calculated expectations of the two rats. Since rewards affect future behavior, the initial running rate of the two animals is the same. In addition, their running rate is slow because they have not been rewarded yet for running. Lines 1660 and 1680 compare the difference between the expectations of rat 1 and rat 2. If rat 1's expectation exceeds rat 2's, the variable S is set equal to 1. If rat 2's expectation is greater than that of rat 1, the variable S is set equal to 2. The variable S now determines which rat has the larger expectation and will get to the goal box first.

Line 1700 calculates the absolute value of the difference between the expectations of the two rats. Lines 1710 through 1730 convert that difference to an integer (I). Lines 1740 through 1755 then set two variables, K(1) and K(2), to values of either 1 or I. Now if rat 1 has a greater expectation than rat 2, rat 1 will move I times for every one time rat 2 moves. If rat 2 has the greater expectation, it will move I times for every one move of rat 1. A total of thirty-four moves is required to move the rats into the goal boxes. The loop for animation begins on line 1780 and ends on line 1920.

The subroutines that do the actual animation (lines 2500–2580 for rat 1; lines 2700 through 2780 for rat 2) are called 34 times. This loop begins on line 1780 and ends on line 1920. Within this loop, two loops exist for animating the two rats. The loop beginning on line 1790 calls the subroutine for animating rat 1 and increments X (the location of rat 1) by five pixels each time it is executed.

The loop beginning on line 1860 calls the subroutine for animating rat 2 and increments Y (the location of rat 2) by five pixels each time it is executed.

Smooth animation is produced in BASIC code by the subroutines located at lines 2500 through 2580 and 2700 through 2780. Lines 2620 and 2720 set HCOLOR equal to black and color over the back portion of the rats. Lines 2540, 2560, 2740, and 2760 return HCOLOR to white and redraw the forward portion of the rat. The locations of the rats are incremented by five pixels each time those subroutines are called. This is a very efficient method for animating in BASIC because a large portion of the animated object does not have to be redrawn on each move. This method is illustrated in Figure 3-1.

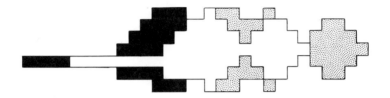

Figure 3-1.   This figure illustrates the animation technique used in program RAT RACE. The area in solid white and solid black is a rat on the screen before an animation step. To move the rat across the screen, light is removed from the pixels in the black area and light is applied to the area covered by dots. Now the white and dotted areas draw a rat on the screen, which has been moved forward five pixels. This technique produces smooth animation using only Applesoft BASIC.

Computations

After the rats both reach their respective goal boxes, program control is returned to line 0260, which calls a computational subroutine located at lines 3000 through 3390. Line 3050 sets F, the rate of learning, to 0.05. Line 3060 begins a two-count loop to calculate expectations for the two rats. Line 3070 calculates the value of obtained reward as the number of pellets (R(P)) times 0.05. Line 3080 calculates the increment in expectation as $E = F(O - E)$. Line 3350 increments the expectation for each rat. Lines 3370 and 3380 print out, at the bottom of the screen, the new value for the expectation of each rat. These values will be used by the animation subroutine to animate the next trial.

Program control now returns to line 0300. The program now asks the user if he wishes to run another trial. If the answer is no, the program jumps to line 480 and ends. If another trial is desired, lines 0340 through 0360 clear the rats out of the goal boxes and return control to line 0160, which begins a new trial by drawing in the runway doors and the rats in the start boxes.

PROGRAM LISTING

```
0010   REM   ************************************************
0020   REM   RAT RACE VERSION 1
0030   REM   ************************************************
0100   CLEAR : HOME
0110   POKE 230,32 : CALL 62450 : HGR
0120   HCOLOR = 3
0150   GOSUB 500
0160   GOSUB 800
0170   GOSUB 1000
0180   GOSUB 1300
0200   PRINT "PRESS ANY KEY TO START   " : GET SS$
0210   HCOLOR = 0
0220   GOSUB 800
0230   GOSUB 1000
0240   HCOLOR = 3
0250   GOSUB 1600
0260   GOSUB 3000
0300   PRINT "DO YOU WANT ANOTHER TRIAL ?"
0310   INPUT SS$
0330   IF SS$ = "NO" THEN GOTO 480
0340   X = 223 : Y = 223 : HCOLOR = 0
0350   GOSUB 2200
0360   HCOLOR = 3
0370   GOTO 160
0480   TEXT : HOME : END
0500   REM   ************************************************
0510   REM   DRAWS RUNWAY 1
0520   HPLOT 220,21 TO 247,21 TO 247,59 TO 220,59 TO 220,53 TO
       69,53 TO 69,59 TO 44,59 TO 44,21 TO 69,21 TO 69,26 TO
       220,26 TO 220,21
0540   HPLOT 221,22 TO 246,22 TO 246,58 TO 221,58 TO 221,52 TO
       68,52 TO 68,58 TO 45,58 TO 45,22 TO 68,22 TO 68,27 TO
       221,27 TO 221,22
0560   HPLOT 245,37 TO 240,37 TO 240,45 TO 245,45
0580   REM   ************************************************
0600   REM   DRAWS RUNWAY 2
0620   HPLOT 220,100 TO 247,100 TO 247,141 TO 220,141 TO 220,134
       TO 69,134 TO 69,141 TO 43,141 TO 43,100 TO 69,100 TO
       69,107 TO 220,107 TO 220,100
0640   HPLOT 221,101 TO 246,101 TO 246,140 TO 221,140 TO 221,133
       TO 68,133 TO 68,140 TO 44,140 TO 44,101 TO 68,101 TO
       68,108 TO 221,108 TO 221,101
0660   HPLOT 245,117 TO 240,117 TO 240,125 TO 245,125
0700   RETURN
0720   REM   ************************************************
0800   REM   DRAWS DOORS RUNWAY 1
0820   HPLOT 68,30 TO 68,49 TO 69,49 TO 69,30 : HPLOT 220,30 TO
       220,49 TO 221,49 TO 221,30
0840   REM   DRAWS DOORS RUNWAY 2
0860   HPLOT 68,111 TO 68,130 TO 69,130 TO 69,111 : HPLOT
       220,111 TO 220,130 TO 221,111 TO 221,130
0880   RETURN
```

```
0900    REM    ***********************************************
1000    REM    DRAWS RAT 1 IN START BOX 1
1020    HPLOT 53,37 TO 55,37 : HPLOT 58,37 : HPLOT 51,38 TO
        59,38 : HPLOT 63,38 TO 64,38 : HPLOT 50,39 TO 60,39 :
        HPLOT 62,39 TO 65,39 : HPLOT 49,40 TO 66,40 : HPLOT
        48,41 TO 60,41 : HPLOT 62,41 TO 65,41
1040    HPLOT 48,42 TO 49,42 : HPLOT 51,42 TO 59,42 : HPLOT 63,42
        TO 64,42 : HPLOT 48,43 : HPLOT 53,43 TO 55,43 : HPLOT
        58,43 : HPLOT 48,44 : HPLOT 48,45 TO 49,45 : HPLOT
        55,45 TO 59,45 : HPLOT 49,46 TO 51,46
1060    HPLOT 54,46 TO 55,46 : HPLOT 51,47 TO 54,47
1080    REM    ***********************************************
1100    REM    DRAWS RAT 2 IN START BOX 2
1120    HPLOT 53,117 TO 55,117 : HPLOT 58,117 : HPLOT 51,118
        TO 59,118 : HPLOT 63,118 TO 64,118 : HPLOT 50,119 TO
        60, 119 : HPLOT 62,119 TO 65,119 : HPLOT 49,120 TO 66,120
        : HPLOT 48,121 TO 60,121 : HPLOT 62,121 TO 65,121
1140    HPLOT 48,122 TO 49,122 : HPLOT 51,122 TO 59,122 : HPLOT
        63,122 TO 64,122 : HPLOT 48,123 : HPLOT 53,123 TO 55,123 :
        HPLOT 58,123 : HPLOT 48,124 : HPLOT 48,125 TO 49,125 :
        HPLOT 55,125 TO 59,125 : HPLOT 49,126 TO 51,126
1160    HPLOT 54,126 TO 55,126 : HPLOT 51,127 TO 54,127
1180    RETURN
1190    REM    ***********************************************
1300    REM    INPUT ROUTINE FOR FOOD PELLETS
1340    FOR B = 1 TO 2
1350    IF B = 1 THEN R$ = "RAT 1"
1360    IF B = 2 THEN R$ = "RAT 2"
1365    PRINT : PRINT : PRINT
1370    VTAB 20
1380    PRINT : PRINT : PRINT
1400    PRINT "HOW MANY PELLETS FOR   "R$" ? (1 TO 20)" :
        INPUT R(B)
1410    IF R(B) > 20 THEN GOTO 1380
1420    IF R(B) < 1 THEN GOTO 1380
1430    PRINT : PRINT : PRINT
1440    NEXT B
1460    RETURN
1480    REM    ***********************************************
1600    REM    ANIMATES RATS
1620    X = 63 : Y = 63
1630    HCOLOR = 3 : GOSUB 2200
1660    IF E(1) > E(2) THEN S = 1
1680    IF E(1) < = E(2) THEN S = 2
1700    D = ABS (E(1) - E(2))
1710    IF D < .01 THEN I = INT (1000*D)
1720    IF D > = .01 THEN I = INT (100 * D)
1730    IF D > .09999 THEN I = INT ( 10 * D )
1740    IF S = 1 THEN K(1) = I + 1
1745    IF S = 1 THEN K(2) = 1
1750    IF S = 2 THEN K(1) = 1
1755    IF S = 2 THEN K(2) = I + 1
1780    FOR C = 1 TO 34
1790    FOR M = 1 to K(1)
1800    IF X > 220 THEN 1820
```

```
1810    GOSUB 2500
1815    X = X + 5
1820    NEXT M
1860    FOR N = 1 TO K(2)
1870    IF Y > 220 THEN 1890
1880    GOSUB 2700
1885    Y = Y + 5
1890    NEXT N
1920    NEXT C
2000    REM   ***************************************************
2200    REM   DRAWS RAT 1 IN RUNWAY 1
2230    HPLOT X + 3,37 TO X + 5,37 : HPLOT X + 8,37 : HPLOT
        X + 1,38 TO X + 9,38 : HPLOT X + 13,38 TO X + 14,38 :
        HPLOT X,39 TO X + 10,39 : HPLOT X + 12,39 TO X + 15, 39 :
        HPLOT X - 1,40 TO X + 16,40 : HPLOT X - 11,41 TO X + 10,41
2250    HPLOT X + 12,41 TO X + 15,41 : HPLOT X -1,42 TO X + 9,42 :
        HPLOT X + 13,42 : HPLOT X + 3,43 TO X + 5,43 : HPLOT
        X + 8,43
2260    REM   ***************************************************
2270    REM   DRAWS RAT 2 IN RUNWAY 2
2300    HPLOT Y + 3,117 TO Y + 5,117 : HPLOT Y + 8,117 :
        HPLOT Y + 1,118 TO Y + 9,118 : HPLOT Y + 13,118 TO
        Y + 14,118 : HPLOT Y,119 TO Y + 10,119 : HPLOT Y + 12,119
        TO Y + 15,119 : HPLOT y - 1,120 TO Y + 16,120 : HPLOT
        Y - 11,121 TO Y + 10,121
2320    HPLOT Y + 12,121 TO Y + 15,121 : HPLOT Y - 1,122 TO
        Y + 9,122 : HPLOT Y + 13,122 : HPLOT Y + 3,123 TO Y +
        5,123 : HPLOT Y + 8,123
2350    RETURN
2360    REM   ***************************************************
2500    REM   ANIMATES RAT 1
2520    HCOLOR = 0 : HPLOT X + 3,37 TO X + 5,37 : HPLOT X + 1,38
        TO X + 5,38 : HPLOT X,39 TO X + 4,39 : HPLOT X - 1,40 TO
        X + 3,40 : HPLOT X - 11,41 TO X - 7,41 : HPLOT X - 1,42
        TO X + 3,42 : HPLOT X + 3,43 TO X + 5,43
2540    HCOLOR = 3 : HPLOT X + 9,37 TO X + 10,37 : HPLOT X +
        13,37 : HPLOT X + 10,38 TO X + 12,38 : HPLOT X + 18,38 TO
        X + 19,38 : HPLOT X + 11,39 : HPLOT X + 17,39 TO X + 20,
        39 : HPLOT X + 17,40 TO X + 21,40 : HPLOT X + 11,41
2560    HPLOT X + 17, 41 TO X + 20,41 : HPLOT X + 10,42 TO X
        + 12,42 : HPLOT X + 18,42 TO X + 19,42 : HPLOT X + 9,43 TO
        X + 10,43 : HPLOT X + 13,43
2580    RETURN
2600    REM   ***************************************************
2700    REM   ANIMATES RAT 2
2720    HCOLOR = 0 : HPLOT Y + 3,117 TO Y + 5,117: HPLOT Y + 1,
        118 TO Y + 5,118 : HPLOT Y,119 TO Y + 4,119 : HPLOT
        Y -1,120 TO Y + 3,120 : HPLOT Y - 11,121 TO Y -7,121 :
        HPLOT Y -1,122 TO Y + 3,122 : HPLOT Y + 3,123 TO Y + 5,123
2740    HCOLOR = 3 : HPLOT Y + 9,117 TO Y + 10,117 : HPLOT Y
        + 13,117 : HPLOT Y + 10,118 TO Y + 12,118 : HPLOT Y + 18,
        118 TO Y + 19,118 : HPLOT Y + 11,119 : HPLOT Y + 17,119
        TO Y + 20,119 : HPLOT Y + 17,120 TO Y + 21,120 : HPLOT
        Y + 11,121
```

```
2760    Y + 17,121 TO Y + 20,121 : HPLOT Y + 10,122 TO Y +
        12,122 : HPLOT Y + 18,122 TO Y + 19,122 : HPLOT Y + 9,
        123 TO Y + 10,123 : HPLOT Y + 13,123
2780    RETURN
2800    REM   *******************************************************
3000    REM   CALCULATION ROUTINE
3060    FOR P = 1 TO 2
3070    O(P) = R(P) * .05
3080    DE(P) = .15 * (O(P) - E(P))
3300    REM   *******************************************************
3310    REM   STORAGE ROUTINE
3350    E(P) = E(P) + DE(P)
3360    NEXT P
3370    PRINT "EXPECTATION OF RAT 1 IS NOW  "E(1)
3380    PRINT "EXPECTATION OF RAT 2 IS NOW  "E(2)
3390    RETURN
3400    REM   *******************************************************
```

APPLICATIONS, EXAMPLES, ILLUSTRATIONS

Program RAT RACE can be used by anyone wanting to learn the rule describing the development of expectations of reward, or the relationship between amount of reward and expectations. Consider, for example, a procedure in which each rat receives a different quantity of reward. The rat in the top runway is given five food pellets every time it scampers down the runway, and the bottom rat gets ten pellets. Figure 3-2 shows that by the third time they run the runway, when the second rat has reached the goal area the first rat is only halfway down the runway. In the bottom portion of Figure 3-2, each rat has had six trials. The rat in the top runway received five pellets each trial and the bottom rat received ten pellets. When the ten-pellet rat reaches the goal area, the five-pellet rat is only about one third of the way down the runway. Larger rewards produce larger expectations.

At the end of each trial, program RAT RACE prints the numerical value of the expectation of each rat at the bottom of the screen. It is zero on the first trial and increases with each rewarded run down the alleyway. The amount of increase, however, gets smaller and smaller each time the reward occurs. This captures our notion of surprisingness. The program user can write down the accumulated value of the expectation after each trial and use these numbers to construct a learning curve on graph paper.

The best way to make a learning curve is to plot trials on the horizontal axis (abscissa) and the accumulated value of expectation on the vertical axis (ordinate). Next, mark the value of expectation above each trial. Connecting these points yields a learning curve. A learning curve also clearly shows that the largest changes in behavior are produced the first few times reward occurs. Successive rewards produce smaller and smaller changes in behavior.

RAT RACE 1 should only be used to study increases in expectations that

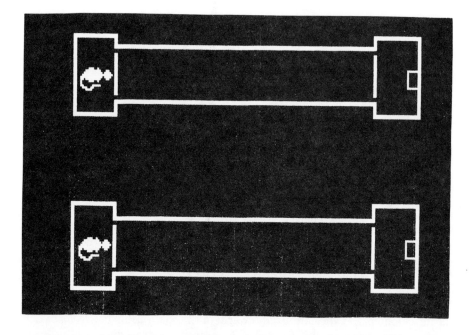

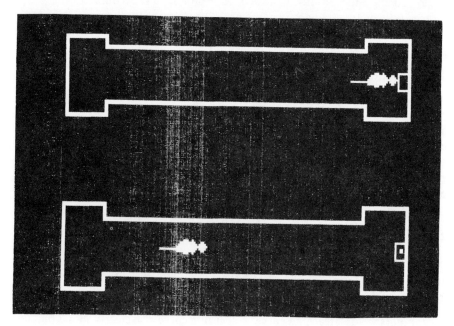

Figure 3-2.   The rat in the top runway in each screen display is receiving five food pellets each time it runs the runway. The bottom rat is receiving ten pellets. This figure shows the relative position of two rats on trials 3 (top display) and 6 (bottom display).

occur as a function of successive rewards, and comparisons between different amounts of reward. Removal of reward, or changes in the amount of the reward, frequently produce frustration. We will incorporate frustration into the program in the next chapter. Since RAT RACE 1 is designed only to illustrate the development of expectations, further discussion of applications of the program must await the incorporation of frustration and courage into the model.

SUMMARY

Rewards are most effective at changing behavior when they are surprising. They are least effective when they are not surprising. The larger the reward, the larger the change in behavior. These facts are captured by the rule that changes in behavior are a constant fraction of the difference between obtained and expected reward: $\Delta E + = F(O - E+)$. One of the most common procedures for studying the relationship between reward and behavior is giving food to a hungry laboratory rat after it runs an alleyway, and measuring changes in the rat's running speed. Program RAT RACE 1 simulates this laboratory preparation and the rule describing changes in expectations. The program user can repeatedly run two rats down alleyways and reward them with food. The program demonstrates the effects of two different reward magnitudes by varying the speed with which the two rats run the runway relative to one another. It also demonstrates the increases in running speed that occur as a function of repeated reward.

ADDITIONAL READINGS

The first reference provides an excellent introduction to the implications of the relationships between behavior and its consequences (rewards, punishment, etc.) for an understanding of human affairs. A brief, but exacting, scholarly, and insightful discussion for the advanced reader is provided in the second reference.

1. Skinner, B. F., *Science and Human Behavior* (New York: Macmillan, 1953).
2. Skinner, B. F., "Selection by Consequences," *Science*, 1981, *213*, pp. 501–4.

The following book chapter, while somewhat technical, provides a thorough introduction to the development of the formula used to model expectations in program RAT RACE.

3. Rescorla, R. A., and Wagner, A. R., "A Theory of Pavlovian Conditioning: Variations in the Effectiveness of Reinforcement and Nonreinforcement," in A. H. Black and W. F. Prokasy, *Classical Conditioning II* (New York: Appleton-Century-Crofts , 1972), pp. 64–99.

This is a very important article for anyone interested in the actual application of our knowledge about the affect of rewards on behavior to human affairs. It discusses some of the frequently unwanted side effects of changes in rewarded behavior. The reference list in this paper also contains a long list of books and articles dealing with the application of reward training to real human situations.

4. Balsam, P. D. and Bondy, A. S., "The Negative Side Effects of Reward," *Journal of Applied Behavior Analysis,* 1983, *16,* pp. 283-96.

4

FRUSTRATION
Program
RAT RACE 2

In Chapter 3, we learned to translate the rules for the development of expectations into an equation. We then used the equation in a computer program that models a hungry rat running an alleyway for food pellets. The equation says that changes in expectations of reward are equal to a constant fraction of the difference between obtained reward and current expectations of reward, $\Delta E+ = F(O - E+)$. In RAT RACE 1, if the rat doesn't obtain the reward he expects, his expectations decrease. In this case, $O - E+$ is negative and $\Delta E+$ is negative. Accordingly, the rat's expectation of reward decreases.

However, most of us know from our everyday experiences that if reward is less than we expected we don't just lower our expectation. We also are frustrated by situations in which rewards don't occur, or are less than we expected. If we expect to get candy from a vending machine and don't, we are frustrated. If we expect to go skiing and it hasn't snowed, we are frustrated. Similarly, if the rat expects to get food at the end of the alleyway and doesn't, he is frustrated. Our model must incorporate this new rule. When reward is less than expectations, two things happen: first, expectations of reward decrease; and second, frustration increases. In this chapter, we will incorporate frustration and its behavioral consequences into program RAT RACE.

Consider, for example, the person at the candy machine who fully expects a chocolate bar ($E+ = 100$). If he puts his two quarters in the slot and fails to receive the chocolate bar, then:

$$\Delta E+ = F(O - E+)$$

$$\Delta E+ = 0.1(0 - 100)$$

$$\Delta E+ = 0.1(-100)$$

$$\Delta E+ = -10$$

The change in expectations is negative and $E+$, the expectation of a chocolate bar, is reduced ten units.

Line 1420 in program RAT RACE 1 does not allow the variable "number of food pellets" to be 0. You can allow 0 food pellets, however, by simply deleting line 1420. Once this change is made, it is possible for the rat to run down the runway and find no food. The effects of no reward can now be simulated by first rewarding the rat with food, and then later omitting food.

If you play with this modification, you will find that larger expectations take longer to reduce to 0 than do smaller expectations. RAT RACE 1 clearly predicts that expectations acquired with large rewards take more trials to approach 0, or take longer to change, than expectations acquired with small rewards. This prediction is not consistent with a well-established rule in behavior research that states that just the opposite is true: behaviors learned with large rewards change more quickly than those learned with small rewards. Obviously, this rule must be incorporated into our equation and computer program.

Now imagine a person who is actually hungry for a candy bar. He has always obtained a chocolate bar after placing two quarters in the candy machine. So he approaches the candy machine, places two quarters in the slot, and then presses the button for the chocolate bar. But nothing happens. He presses the coin return, gets the quarters back, and starts over. He still doesn't get a chocolate bar. Next, he beats on the side of the machine with his fist. Some people even start kicking the machine. Unfulfilled expectations are frustrating and aggression is frequently a behavioral consequence of frustration.

It is possible to study frustration with the laboratory model of a hungry rat running a runway. If the rat first experiences food for running and then receives no food for running, he behaves in a manner similar to the human at the candy machine. If the rat has learned to expect food in the goal box and doesn't get it, he frequently hisses, bites things, or tries to escape from the runway. He shows all of the behavioral evidence of being frustrated. And the greater his expectation for food, the greater his frustration when he doesn't get it.

Frustration has very clear behavioral consequences. Some of the behaviors it produces are aggression, escape, daydreaming, and regression to previously learned behavior. All of these behaviors interfere with the original behavior— approaching the candy machine, or running the runway. The fact that behaviors produced by frustration interfere with the original learned behavior makes it easy to incorporate frustration into our simulation.

First, however, let's examine what this analysis of frustrative nonreward means for the ease of changing rewarded behaviors. Behaviors learned with large rewards produce large expectations of reward. Consequently, when reward does not occur, there is a large amount of frustration and a large amount of interference with the learned behavior. This interference lowers the rate of the originally learned behavior. The expectation of reward is overcome by the large amount of frustration. This analysis suggests a rather different effect of no reward when the expectation of reward is low. In this case, the amount of frustration is low. The amount of frustration that interferes with the original behavior is low. The new rule for our model is: The greater the expectation, the greater the frustration when the expectation is not fulfilled.

Nonreward when reward is expected is not the only situation that is frustrating. In fact, any time the quantity $O - E+$ is negative (when obtained reward is smaller than the expectation of reward), frustration occurs. If the person approaches the candy machine expecting to get a chocolate bar for two quarters and the machine takes his money but dispenses only a single jellybean, the person will be frustrated. Any situation is frustrating when obtained reward is less than expected reward. And this frustration is detrimental to learned behavior.

The following example illustrates the effect of shifting from large to small reward. Consider two rats, one learning to run the runway for a reward of twenty pellets and the second for five pellets. If after we first give both of these rats sixty trials and then change the twenty-pellet reward to five pellets, the results are very interesting. The rat whose reward was decreased from twenty pellets to five pellets will begin to run more slowly than the rat that always received five pellets. Since the experience of receiving a large reward followed by a small reward typically depresses behavior below the level appropriate to the small reward, psychologists refer to this phenomenon as a depression effect. This effect is frequently temporary.

Incorporation of the consequences of frustrative reward reductions (rewards that are smaller than expected) into our model is straightforward. The behavior of the rat is subdivided into two classes. First, the rat can approach the goal area of the runway on the basis of her expectation of reward $(E+)$. Second, she can avoid the goal area of the runway as a consequence of her expectation of frustration or reward reductions $(E-)$. The formula for changes in behavior is the same in both cases. The formula describes changes in behavior based on frustrative nonreward as well as behavior based on reward. We now apply the same formula to changes in expectation of nonreward, $E-$, as well as changes in expectation of reward, $E+$. To calculate running speed, or animation rate, we subtract the interfering avoidance behaviors from the approach behaviors.

EXPANDING THE MODEL

Our model now includes changes in two classes of behavior, approach and avoidance, that occur as a function of two classes of events, reward and reward reductions. The expanded model is summarized in Table 4-1.

Approach–Reward

$$\Delta E+ = F(O - E+)$$

Changes in the expectation of a reward are a fraction of the difference between obtained and expected reward. If reward occurs, expectations increase. This is the formula presented in Chapter 3.

Approach–Reward Reduction

$$\Delta E+ = F(O - E+)$$

When obtained reward is less than expected reward, obtained minus expected reward $(O - E+)$ is negative and the calculated change in $E+$ is negative. The expectation of reward decreases.

TABLE 4-1

Behavior

	Approach	Avoidance

	Approach	Avoidance
Reward	$\Delta E+ \; = \; F(O \; - \; E+)$ Increases expectations	$\Delta E- \; = \; F(O \; - \; E-)$ Decreases frustration
No Reward	$\Delta E+ \; = \; F(O \; - \; E+)$ Decreases expectations	$\Delta E- \; = \; F(E+ \; - \; E-)$ Increases frustration

Consequences

The general formula is $\Delta E \; = \; F(O \; - \; E)$.

The amount of behavior change that occurs on a single trial is a constant fraction (F) of the difference between the maximum change the obtained reward will produce (O) and the existing expectation (E).

Avoidance–Reward Reduction

$$\Delta E- \; = \; F(E+ \; - \; E-)$$

This formula is used whenever $O - E+$ is negative. It calculates changes in the tendency to avoid the site of reward that are produced by frustration. The maximum amount of frustration ($E-$) that can occur depends on the amount of expectation ($E+$) that is already learned. When expectations are large and reward is less than expected (including no reward) the individual is frustrated. His or her tendency to avoid the goal object is therefore increased. When expectations are low and reward is less than expected, the individual is not as frustrated. Experiences in which obtained reward is less than expected reward produce increases in the tendency to avoid the goal object according to the formula $\Delta E- \; = \; F(E+ \; - \; E-)$.

To incorporate frustration into our computer simulation we must implement three additional steps. Before any calculations occur, we must first check to see if $O - E+$ is positive or negative. If $O - E+$ is negative we must calculate decreases in expectation and increases in frustration. If $O - E+$ is positive we must calculate increases in expectation and decreases in frustration. Then we must subtract any avoidance tendencies due to frustration from approach tendencies due to expectations to obtain a quantity to use for animation rate.

Avoidance–Reward

$$\Delta E- = F(O - E-)$$

A rewarded experience has the effect of reducing expectations of nonreward (accumulated or learned frustration). In this case, reward is greater than expectations. Recall that $E-$ has a negative value with respect to running speed. Therefore, decreases in frustration that occur on rewarded trials reduce the amount of interfering frustration. Application of this formula has the effect of making $E-$ a smaller negative number—that is, reducing avoidance behavior. It reduces the expectation of nonreward and its effects of avoiding the goal. Even if some avoidance tendency existed, a series of rewarded experiences would bring them close to zero.

BEHAVIORAL PHENOMENA SIMULATED BY RAT RACE 2

Frustration

RAT RACE 1 simulates the behavioral consequences of expectations by having two hungry rats approach the ends of two runways at a speed that varies with their expectations. The rat with the largest expectation gets to the goal area first. Increases in expectations produce increases in the speed of approaching the food cup. RAT RACE 2 adds a new component called frustration by utilizing the fact that behaviors produced by frustration interfere with running. Frustration is conceptualized, for purposes of the simulation, as a class of behaviors that counteract the tendency to approach the food cup in the runway. Frustration results in behavior that avoids the site of frustration. Indeed, one of the most common behavioral consequences of frustration is escape from the source of frustration.

In program RAT RACE 2, any time obtained reward is less than expected reward ($O - E+$ is negative), frustration is increased and the rat's speed of approaching the food cup is decreased.

Resistance to Change

Changes in behavior require two processes. First, an existing behavior must decrease in frequency. Second, new behaviors must be learned. This program allows us to simulate the effects of reward reductions and zero reward on previously rewarded behavior. Not rewarding learned behaviors produces the decrease in existing behaviors essential to the process of change.

Behaviors learned with large rewards decrease under conditions of no reward at a rate faster than behaviors learned under small reward. The effects of frustration on resistance to change accounts for these facts. RAT RACE 2 simulates the facts that behavior learned under large reward conditions go away faster than those learned under small reward when reward is no longer given.

Depression

Reductions in reward to amounts below what an individual expects typically depress behavior to very low levels. Shifts from large to small rewards produce rates of behavior lower than the rates produced by small rewards. This type of temporary depression effect is also simulated by RAT RACE 2.

DESCRIPTION OF PROGRAM RAT RACE 2

RAT RACE 1 accurately simulates changes in expectation of reward whenever the reward is greater than or equal to the expectation of reward. In addition, RAT RACE 2 simulates changes in frustration when the reward is smaller than the expectation. In order to simulate expectation and frustration, the computations become slightly more elaborate. The computational subroutine must first calculate whether the obtained reward is greater than or less than the expected reward. If $O>E$, an increase in expectation must be calculated and a decrease in frustration. If $O<E$, an increase in learned frustration must be calculated and a decrease in expectation. These changes in expectation and frustration must then be added to the accumulated values of expectation and frustration. Accumulated frustration must be subtracted from accumulated expectation to obtain a value that most directly represents the running speed of the rat. In addition to these changes in the computational subroutine, some embellishments will be added to the program.

Computational Subroutine

A new set of variables has been introduced in this version of the program. They will be used throughout the remainder of the book.

E1–changes in expectation of reward
E2–changes in expectation of frustration
T1–accumulated expectation of reward
T2–accumulated expectation of frustration
T4–difference between T1 and T2

The variable T4 will be used for calculating the animation rate. The rate is calculated by subtracting accumulated frustration from accumulated expectation after each trial. T4 will reflect both expectations of reward and the interfering effects of expectations of frustration.

The following changes must be made in RAT RACE 1:

1. DELETE LINE 1420

2. CHANGE LINE 1400 to

```
1400   PRINT "HOW MANY PELLETS FOR "R$" ?

(0 TO 20)":INPUT R(B)
```

Line 1420 restricted version 1 from accepting an input value of 0 food pellets. By deleting the program line, the user may now input 0 food pellets. Line 1400 changes the input prompt line to read 0 TO 20 instead of 1 TO 20.

3. DELETE LINES 1660, 1680, 1700.

4. ADD:

```
1660   IF T4(1) > T4(2) THEN S=1

1680   IF T4(1) < = T4(2) THEN S=2


1700   D = ABS (T4(1) - T4(2))
```

These line numbers were used in version 1 to compare the expectations of the two rats for purposes of determining animation rate. These new line numbers simply replace the variable E1 (expectation of reward) with T4 (expectation of reward minus frustration).

5. DELETE LINES 3000 to 3400.

6. ADD:

```
3000   REM   CALCULATION
3010   REM   ROUTINE
3060   FOR P = 1 TO 2
3070   O(P) = R(P) * .05
3080   IF O(P) < T1(P) THEN GOTO 3200
3090   REM   ****************************
3100   REM   WHEN O > T1
```

```
3110   REM   INCREMENTS E1
3120   E1(P) = .15 * (O(P) - T1(P))
3130   IF T2(P) < = 0 THEN GOTO 3300
3140   REM   DECREMENTS E2
3150   E2(P) = .05 * (0 - T2(P))

3180   GOTO 3300
3190   REM   *****************************
3200   REM   WHEN 0 < T1
3210   REM   INCREMENTS E2
3220   OX(P) = ABS (2 * (O(P) - T1(P)))
3230   E2(P) = .15 * (OX(P) - T2(P))
3240   IF T1(P) < 0 THEN GOTO 3300
3250   REM   DECREMENTS E1
3260   E1(P) = .05 * (O(P) - T1(P))
3270   REM   *****************************
3300   REM   ACCUMULATES E'S
3310   T1(P) = (T1(P) + E1(P))
3320   T2(P) = (T2(P) + E2(P))
3330   T4(P) = (T4(P) + (E1(P) - E2(P)))
3400   NEXT P
3490   REM   *****************************
3500   PRINT "EXPECTATION OF RAT 1 IS "T4(1)
3510   PRINT "EXPECTATION OF RAT 2 IS "T4(2)
3600   RETURN
4000   REM   *****************************
```

Lines 3000 through 3600 are the new computational subroutine for the model. Obtained rewards must now be divided into two classes: those that are greater than expectations, and those that are less than expectations. This is done in line 3080. If obtained reward (O) is less than the accumulated expectation of reward, frustration occurs. In this case, frustration must be increased and expectation decreased. These calculations are carried out in lines 3200 through 3260. Since the amount of frustration depends on the magnitude of the discrepancy between obtained and expected reward, this calculation is carried out on line 3220. The value is assigned to the variable OX. Since the negative discrepancy between obtained and expected reward is the basis for frustration, OX is used in place of O in our general formula $E = F(O - E)$ for calculating increases in frustration. The increase in frustration is calculated on line 3230. The decrease in expectation is calculated on line 3260.

In the event that obtained reward exceeds the expectation of reward, increments in expectation and decrements in frustration are calculated on lines 3120 and 3150, respectively. Lines 3310 and 3320 accumulate the changes in expectations and frustration to new variables T1 and T2. Line 3330 calculates accumulated expectation minus accumulated frustration (T4). Since frustration-produced behaviors interfere with approaching the reward, T4 is the variable that is now used to determine the speed of running the runway.

Dispensing of Food Pellets

Version 2 of program RAT RACE is also modified to depict the placing of food pellets into the goal area of the runway. Lines 4000 through 4200 make up the subroutine called from the input routine for the number of food pellets. Lines 1887 through 1830 remove the pellets when the rat reaches the goal box.

7. ADD:

```
1425   GOSUB 4000

4010   REM   DISPENSES PELLETS
4020   IF B = 2 THEN GOTO 4050
4030   Z1 = 40:Z2 = 41
4040   GOTO 4100
4050   Z1 = 120:Z2 = 121
4100   FOR A = 1 TO R(B)
4110   FOR G = 1 TO 5
4120   X = PEEK ( - 16330)
4130   NEXT G
4140   HCOLOR = 3: HPLOT 243,Z1 TO 243,Z2 TO
       244,Z2 TO 244,Z1
4150   FOR H = 1 TO 25
4160   NEXT H
4170   HCOLOR = 0: HPLOT 243,Z1 TO 243,Z2 TO
       244,Z2 TO 244,Z1
4180   NEXT A
4190   HCOLOR = 3: HPLOT 243,Z1 TO 243,Z2 TO
       244,Z2 TO 244,Z1
4200   RETURN


1817   GOTO 1830
1820   HCOLOR = 0:HPLOT 243,40 TO 243,41 TO
       244,41 TO 244,40:HCOLOR=3
1830   NEXT M

1887   GOTO 1900
1890   HCOLOR = 0:HPLOT 243,120 TO 243,121 TO
       244,121 TO 244,120:HCOLOR=3
1900   NEXT N
```

EXAMPLES AND ILLUSTRATIONS

We use RAT RACE 2 just like RAT RACE 1. The program user types in the amount of food reward for each of the rats before they run the runway. However, the food pellets are now dispensed into the food cup with visual and auditory feedback to the user. After the food is dispensed, pressing any key will open the start-box and goal-box doors and the rats will run down the runway. Which rat reaches the goal box first is now determined by the amount of expectation minus the amount of interfering frustration. The effects of frustration are only indirectly demonstrated in the animated behavior of the rat. Frustration is simply subtracted from expectation to obtain a value that accurately reflects the speed with which the rat runs the runway. Since version 2 of this program now includes frustration, the program accurately depicts the behavioral consequences of no reward when reward is expected, and reductions in the amount of reward.

Resistance to Change

In order for a new behavior to be learned, the present behavior must be eliminated. The rate with which rewarded behaviors go away when reward is no longer available is inversely related to the amount of reward given during the original learning.

Figure 4-1 shows plots of the values of T4, learned expectation minus learned frustration, for a sample output of RAT RACE 2. The value on vertical axis T4, learned expectation minus learned frustration, is used by the animation algorithm to determine which rat gets to the goal box first. This value is displayed at the bottom of the screen after each run down the runway. This example begins by dispensing ten pellets into the food cup for the first rat and five pellets

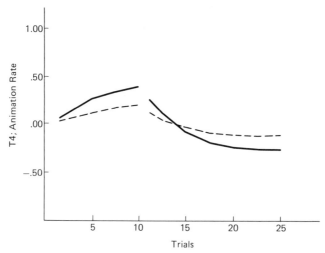

Figure 4-1. Trials 1 through 10 were followed by ten pellets of food for one simulated rat (solid line) and five pellets of food for the other rat (broken line). Neither simulated rat received any food on trials 15 through 20. Notice the crossover on trial 14. From trial 14 on, the rat that received ten pellets on trials 1 through 10 ran more slowly than the rat that received five pellets. This simulation illustrates the frustrating effect of nonreward when reward is expected.

for the second rat. They then run down the runway, eat the food, and the value of T4 is calculated and displayed at the bottom of the screen. That value is then plotted for trial 1 for each of the two rats. This is repeated for ten trials. The rat receiving ten pellets acquired a greater expectation of reward and got to the goal box sooner than the rat receiving five pellets. Beginning with the eleventh trial, neither rat was given any food after scampering down the runway. This was done in order to demonstrate how quickly the running behavior goes away when reward is no longer available. As you can see, by the fourth no-food trial (trial 14) the rat that learned to run for five pellets has a larger total expectation (T4) and therefore gets to the goal sooner than the one trained with ten pellets. This difference continues to increase until the fifteenth no food trial. Recall that this is happening because the rat trained with the larger food reward is experiencing a larger amount of frustration. Frustration interferes with running. This example illustrates the surprising fact that behaviors learned with large rewards are less resistant to change than behaviors learned with small rewards.

Depression Effects

Figure 4-2 illustrates the depression effect that occurs when reward is reduced from twenty food pellets to five food pellets. During the first ten trials, one rat was fed twenty food pellets each time it reached the goal. The second rat was fed five pellets. Beginning on the eleventh trial, both rats were given five pellets each time they ran the runway. While one might expect that the rat that is shifted from twenty pellets to five pellets will run at the same speed as the one

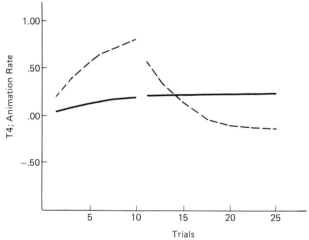

Figure 4-2. Graph of a depression effect. On trials 1 through 10, one rat received twenty pellets reward (broken line) and the second rat received five pellets (solid line). On trials 11 through 25 both rats received five pellets after running the runway. Notice that the animal that was shifted from twenty pellets to five pellets runs much slower than a rat who has always received five pellets. Since behavior is depressed below the level normally maintained by five pellets of food this is called a depression effect.

always given five pellets, this is not what happens. You can see in Figure 4-2 that by the fifteenth trial the rat given five pellets all along is reaching the goal sooner than the one shifted from twenty to five. Since the rate of running is depressed below the level appropriate to five pellets, we call this a *depression effect*. You can observe this depression effect with the program by simply feeding one rat the same small number of food pellets on each trial and giving the other rat a series of large rewards followed by a series of small rewards.

You will notice in Figure 4-2 that by about the twenty-fifth trial the shifted rat is starting to return to the level of T4 shown by the unchanged five-pellet rat. Actually, this return to the level appropriate to five food pellets occurs sooner than RAT RACE 2 demonstrates. When rewarded with five food pellets for running, even when expecting to be frustrated, the shifted rat learns courage to approach the goal box in the presence of frustration behaviors. However, we will not incorporate courage into the program until the next chapter. You will see that after courage is incorporated into the program these depression effects are only temporary.

Program RAT RACE 2 demonstrates some surprising effects of reward on behavior. First, behaviors learned with large rewards can be changed much quicker than behaviors learned with small rewards. Second, reductions in the amount of reward depress behaviors to a level below that appropriate to the new small reward. These facts, and others, can be seen by using the RAT RACE 2 computer program.

The depression effect, and our demonstrations of resistance to change as a function of reward amount, may help explain many puzzling aspects of life. Sometimes, for example, we might offer the teenager next door eight dollars to cut the grass. He stops working in the middle of the job, however, and doesn't finish cutting the grass. We are puzzled by his behavior because he was told he would get eight dollars when the job was finished. However, unknown to us, perhaps his father gives him twenty dollars for cutting the lawn. Clearly, the eight dollars is a reduction in reward and depresses behavior. Try to think of other instances in your life in which you were puzzled by behavior that you may now be able to describe as depression effects, or resistance to change phenomena.

By this time, many applications of this computer program are probably becoming obvious. It can be used by people who are involved in changing behavior (therapists, educators, clergy) to learn about the effects of reward on behavior. The equations can be incorporated into computer games, computer operating systems, and robotics to produce more life-like characters. Again, however, we will delay a substantial discussion of applications until the end of the next chapter, when we have incorporated courage into the program. At that point, we will have a model that simulates many complex behaviors, and a large measure of confidence that it can simulate a surprisingly wide variety of psychological phenomena. It will be more appropriate then to discuss applications.

EXTENSIONS AND IMPROVEMENTS

Program RAT RACE is designed to be understood by a variety of people who are interested in computers and/or psychology. For those with more technical expertise in computing, there are ways in which the program can be extended and improved.

Frustration is not directly depicted in the behavior of the rats in RAT RACE 2. The amount of frustration the animal has learned is subtracted from his expectations to obtain a quantity to use for animation of running speed. This procedure is based on the observation that frustration produces behavior that interferes with running. Yet those behaviors could be illustrated directly. Typical frustration-produced behaviors in rats include hissing, rearing, biting, digging, and head turning. Animation routines can be written to show these behaviors. The variable T1 can be used for running behavior, and T2 for frustration behavior. The animation algorithm could then call either running behavior or frustration behavior with probabilities related to their calculated values. Such an improvement in the program would more accurately represent our knowledge of behavior.

Most frustration behavior has the property of avoiding the source of frustration. Indeed, rewards that are less than expected are sometimes so aversive that rats will learn to escape them. The way that we have examined this in the laboratory is to place a new box beside the goal box and reduce the wall height between the goal box and this new box. When frustration is large, rats will learn to jump across the wall into the new box to escape the frustrating situation. This behavior could also be simulated in the program.

The present animation algorithm was chosen because of the desire to provide program listings to computer users who are familiar with BASIC but who are not knowledgeable about shape tables or the 6502 machine language. It is possible to rewrite program RAT RACE using shape tables and machine language to allow the animation algorithm to more directly reflect each rat's accumulated expectation and frustration. The present algorithm simply compares the two values of T4 and the number of moves each rat makes relative to the other (on each animation step) is a function of the difference between the two values. This technique can be improved on by using other programming tools and techniques.

SUMMARY

This chapter began by noting that if reward is expected and does not occur, frustration results. Frustration produces behaviors that interfere with running the runway. Frustration, like expectations, is learned. The amount of change in frustration that results when reward is less than expected is calculated using the same formula we used for changes in expectation: $\Delta E+ = F(O-E+)$. We now use $E-$ to symbolize frustration and its behaviors and write our formula as $\Delta E- = F(E+ -E-)$: increments in frustration are a constant fraction of the difference between the expectation of reward and the amount of frustration already expected (learned). Table 4-1 summarizes the form of the formula used for changes in expectations of frustration under conditions of reward and reward reduction. Program RAT RACE was then revised to incorporate frustration and to show the dispensing of food pellets.

RAT RACE 2 now depicts the fact that frustration interacts with expectations to produce an inverse relationship between reward magnitude and resistance to change. The program also clearly simulates depression effects that occur when reward is smaller than expected.

ADDITIONAL READINGS

The first three references provide detailed descriptions of our knowledge of frustrating events and their effects on behavior.

1. Amsel, A., "Behavioral Habituation, Counterconditioning, and a General Theory of Persistence," in A. H. Black and W. F. Prokasy (eds.), *Classical Conditioning II* (New York: Appleton-Century-Crofts, 1972).
2. Daly, H. B., "Learning of a Hurdle Jump Response to Escape Cues Paired with Reduced Reward or Frustrative Nonreward," *Journal of Experimental Psychology,* 1969, *79,* 146–57.
3. Daly, H. B., "Reinforcing Properties of Escape from Frustration Aroused in Various Learning Situations," in G. H. Bower (ed.), *The Psychology of Learning and Motivation,* Vol. 8, (New York: Academic Press, 1974).

The following paper (and others it refers to) contains research data demonstrating the effects of frustrative nonreward on human behavior.

4. Newberry, B. H., "Response Variability and the Partial Reinforcement Effect," *Journal of Experimental Psychology,* 1971, *89,* 137–41.

5

LEARNING TO BE COURAGEOUS

Program RAT RACE 3

In Chapter 3, we began developing a model of the effects of rewards on behavior. Rewards increase the expectation of reward and in RAT RACE 1 we simulated the development of expectations. In Chapter 4, we expanded our model to include the frustrating effects of rewards that are smaller than expectations. RAT RACE 2 simulates both the development of expectations and frustration. In this chapter, we will consider what happens when an individual has both expectations of reward and frustration and then obtains reward. In a word, he learns courage—the tendency to approach the site of reward even when it might result in frustration. Program RAT RACE 3 will then be able to simulate a wide variety of experiences we have in rewarding and nonrewarding environments.

When we last imagined the person in front of the candy machine, he was kicking and cursing it for failing to dispense the chocolate bar he expected. Now he is in the airport lobby at three o'clock in the morning. The coffee shop doesn't open for two more hours, and he hasn't eaten since noon the day before. He is sitting in a chair looking at the candy machine. The candy machine did not yield any chocolate when he last put quarters in the slot. He tilted it, hit it, kicked it, and begged it. Now his stomach growls. He can't decide whether it is grumbling because he is hungry or because he is mad at the machine. He slowly rises from the chair and walks over to the candy machine. He casually puts two quarters in the slot and pushes the button for the chocolate bar. Click, click, clunk. A chocolate bar slides down the chute and stops at the lip of the tray in front of him. Smiling now, he retrieves the chocolate bar. He returns to his seat, sits down, and enjoys the candy. But what has he learned from this experience? How will this chocolate bar affect his behavior in the future?

We can study these questions using our simple model of a laboratory rat running the runway for food. The rat, like the character in the airport terminal at 3:00 A.M., has few options. He has been running down the runway only to find an empty food dish. He has chewed on the runway walls, hissed at the experimenter, and tried to jump out of the goal box only to find it covered by a plastic cover. Now the researcher has placed the rat in the start box and opened the door. The rat looks down the runway to the goal box. He can't quite see into the food dish. The rat's stomach growls and he can't decide whether this occurs because he is hungry or because he is anticipating being frustrated in the goal box. After a short wait, he begins to wander down the runway, stopping occasionally to wonder. "There's food there—it has been there in the past—run to the food. The dish may be empty, it has happened before. Escape." But eventually he reaches the food cup, which is full of food pellets. The rat smiles, picks them up in his paws, and begins to eat. But what has he learned from this experience? How will these food pellets affect his future behavior?

Our friend in the airport departs on a 7:00 A.M. flight and we are unable to follow him to observe the effect of the chocolate bar on his future behavior. The rat, however, has been returned to the cozy comfort of his home cage in the laboratory and we can observe his future behavior.

RAT RACE 2 can simulate the situation described in these opening paragraphs. What we see in the simulation is simple enough. Rewards increase expectations and decrease frustration. No reward increases frustration and decreases expectations. Consider, for example, what happens if we give one rat food pellets only 50 percent of the time and the other rat found food every time (100 percent) he ran the runway. For the rat given food 50 percent of the time, some trials would increase an expectation of food and others would produce an increase in expectation of frustration. The rat given food 100 percent of the time would only experience increases in expectation. The rat rewarded 100 percent of the time should have a much larger expectation of reward than the one rewarded 50 percent of the time. It should therefore take more trials with zero reward for the running behavior to stop in the 100 percent rat than the 50 percent rat. However, well-documented observations of many animals (including rats, pigeons, monkeys, and humans) has shown that behavior rewarded on a 50 percent schedule persists much longer when reward is no longer available than behavior learned under a schedule of 100 percent reward. This phenomenon is so common that it has a special name—*partial reinforcement extinction effect (PREE)*. The fact that behavior learned under a 50 percent schedule of reward is more persistent when reward is no longer available than behavior learned under a 100 percent schedule of reward (continuous reward) is very important in understanding and changing behavior.

Why is behavior so persistent under partial reward conditions? Think back to the rat approaching the goal box expecting both food and frustration—and receiving food. The rat was rewarded for approaching the goal box when expecting to be frustrated. We created a situation in the laboratory and in our simulation similar to the one in the airport at 3:00 A.M. The individual approached a goal event, even though aware of possible frustration, and was then rewarded. What he learned is courage to act even when anticipating frustration. The maximum amount of courage (C) he can learn depends on the amount of frustration ($E-$) he expects. If his expectation of frustration is large, he will be quite surprised to find the food. Under this condition, there will be a large increment in courage. If his expectation of frustration is small, he won't be as surprised to find the food and there will not be much change in the amount of courage he shows. Learning of all forms follows the general formula $\Delta E = F(O - E)$. Courage can be learned just as expectations and frustration can be learned. But the maximum amount of courage (C) depends on the amount of frustration he expects ($E-$). So the formula for increases in courage is $\Delta C = F(E- - C)$.

We now have a model that contains three psychological constructs—expectation, frustration, and courage. Whenever a reward is greater than its expectation, the expectation is increased according to the formula $\Delta E + = F(O - E +)$. Whenever a reward is less than its expectation, frustration is increased accordingly to the formula $\Delta E - = F(E + - E -)$. Whenever frustration is expected but reward is obtained, courage is increased according to the formula $\Delta C = F(E - - C)$. This model has been found to be consistent with a large number of research findings covering a variety of organisms, situations, and behaviors. It also has been found to be useful when applied to education, daily life, and psychotherapy.

BEHAVIORAL PHENOMENA SIMULATED BY RAT RACE 3

Much to our surprise, behaviors learned under schedules of occasional reward are much more persistent (or resistant to change) when rewards are no longer available than behaviors learned under schedules of continuous reward. For many years, psychologists reasoned that the more a behavior was rewarded the better it was learned. We now know, however, that this is simply not true. In fact, behaviors learned under 50 percent reward schedules are more difficult to change than behaviors that are always followed by reward. This can be simulated with RAT RACE 3.

The model of learning that this program simulates describes many of the fine nuances of behavior changes produced when rewards are shifted back and forth between large and small amounts. It also simulates known effects of gradual reductions in reward and complex sequences of changes in reward amount.

Behaviors that lead first to a large reward and then are followed by a small reward, are depressed below the level appropriate to the small reward. This depression effect was discussed in Chapter 4. If the same behavior is subsequently followed by large reward, the behavior will return to a level above the level appropriate to the large reward. This elation effect can be simulated by RAT RACE 3.

The program also can be used to simulate many of the research findings on the tendency to escape from frustration. Such simulation would require the user to display the values of the variable T2 (frustration) or use it to animate escape behavior as suggested at the end of Chapter 4.

RAT RACE 3 also can be used to simulate a finding experimental psychologists call the *Overlearning Extinction Effect*. The more reward training an individual experiences, the greater the expectation, and therefore the greater the frustration when reward is no longer available. The larger the amount of continuously rewarded training, the faster the behavior will change when reward is no longer available.

If one is interested in producing persistent changes in behavior, RAT RACE will illustrate that a good way to do that is to begin with a 100 percent reward schedule, shift to a 50 percent reward schedule, and then slowly reduce the frequency of reward. Play with the program yourself and see what you can learn about the relationship between behavior and its consequences.

DESCRIPTION OF PROGRAM RAT RACE 3

Two new variables are added to RAT RACE:

E3–changes in courage
T3–accumulated courage

The following changes must be made to RAT RACE.

```
DELETE Line 3340
ADD:
3162    IF T2(P) < = 0 THEN GOTO 3300
3165    REM   INCREMENTS E3
3265    IF T2(P)<=0 THEN GOTO 3300
3170    E3(P) = .15 * (T2(P) - T3(P))
3270    REM   DECREMENTS E3
3280    E3(P) = .05 * (0 - T3(P))
3290    REM ********************
3325    T3(P) = (T3(P) + E3(P))
3340    T4(P) = (T4(P) + (E1(P) - E2(P) + E3(P)))
```

In RAT RACE 3, when obtained reward is greater than expected reward, and when frustration is greater than 0, expectations are increased, frustration is decreased, and courage is increased. Line 3162 checks to see if frustration is greater than zero, and line 3170 increments courage. If obtained reward is less than the expected reward, the expectation of reward must be decreased, frustration increased, and courage decreased. Line 3280 calculates the decrease in courage. Line 3325 accumulates changes in courage (E3) to the variable T3. Line 3340 calculates total accumulated expectation by summing the existing expectation, and changes in expectation, minus changes in frustration, plus changes in courage.

EXAMPLES AND ILLUSTRATIONS

Occasional Reward

Figure 5-1 illustrates a comparison between the resistance to change of behavior always rewarded and behavior rewarded only 50 percent of the time. This graph depicts the total expectation (T4) of two rats. One rat was always given twenty pellets of food for running and the other was given twenty pellets and 0 pellets on alternate runs. Beginning on the twenty-fifth trial neither rat received any more food for running. Notice that by the sixth no-food run (trial 30) the rat who received twenty food pellets on all of the first twenty-four runs has a smaller total expectation than the one who was rewarded half of the time. If you simulate this comparison using the program, you will see that from the sixth no-food trial on, the partially rewarded rat runs faster than the continuously rewarded rat. Behaviors learned under conditions of occasional reward are therefore shown to be more resistant to change than those learned under continuous reward.

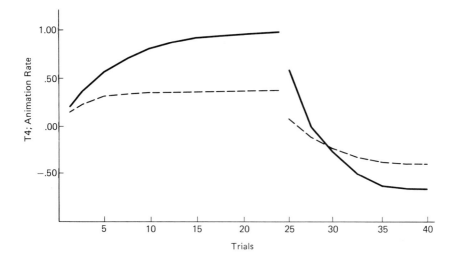

Figure 5-1.   Partial reinforcement extinction effect. On trials 1 through 24, one rat received a reward every time it ran the alleyway (solid line). The second rat (broken line) was only rewarded every other time it ran. On trials 25 through 40, neither rat was rewarded for running. Notice that the rat that was always rewarded runs more slowly from trial 28 on than the rat who was rewarded on only half of the trials.

A familiar example of this from daily life is fishing behavior. Most people can spend many, many hours, and even days of fishing without a bite because they learned to fish under conditions of occasional reward. Imagine instead the following scenario. The first seventy-five times a person goes fishing he catches ten fish in ten casts and goes home. The seventy-sixth time he goes fishing he doesn't get a bite in twenty casts. He is likely to go home. The seventy-seventh, seventy-eighth and seventy-ninth times he goes fishing, he casts ten to fifteen times without a bite. That would probably be so frustrating that he would take up backpacking. But, because most of us actually learned to fish under partial reward conditions we continue to fish. We don't change this behavior very easily.

Elation

Just as the word *depression* refers to responding that is below the level normally supported by a particular reward, the word *elation* refers to responding above the level normally supported by a particular reward. RAT RACE 2 demonstrates that a shift from a large reward to a small reward will produce depression. A change from a small reward to a large reward does not always, however, produce an elation effect. In order for elation to reliably occur, there must be some way for approach strength to exceed the limit set by the reward. Under some conditions, program RAT RACE 3 will produce a total expectation of reward and courage that exceeds the limit set by the number of food pellets. To illustrate, first give both rats a series of about ten runs with twenty food pellets each run. Then shift one rat to five pellets for ten trials while continuing to give the other rat twenty pellets. Now shift the first rat back to twenty pellets. By the fourteenth trial of this last phase, you will see that the total expectation of the first rat exceeds the expectation of the second rat. The rat that receives the sequence of large-small-large rewards will have an expectation that exceeds one, the maximum set by the twenty pellets. This elation effect is produced by the program in the following way: During the first ten large-reward trials, expectation becomes quite large, approaching the limit of one set by the twenty pellets. During the next ten five-pellet-trials frustration is accumulated because obtained reward is less than expected reward. Now shift back to twenty

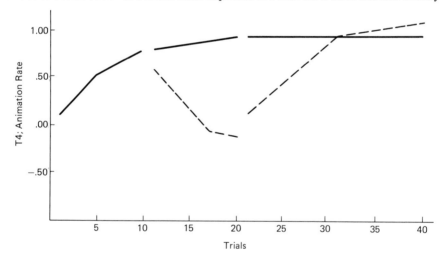

Figure 5-2. Illustration of an elation effect. On trials 1 through 40, one rat received the large reward everytime it ran the alleyway (solid line). The second rat (broken line) received the large reward on trials 1 through 10 and the two lines are the same. On trials 11 to 20, the second rat received a small reward and on trials 26 to 40 it received the large reward again. Notice that beginning on about trial 30 the rat that has experienced the reward sequence large to small to large runs faster than the rat that has always received the large reward. This difference on trials 30 to 40 is an elation effect.

pellets per run. During these trials, obtained reward is greater than expected reward, which was reduced during the five-pellet runs. Since frustration that was learned during the five-pellet runs is also present, courage will be learned. It is the summation of expectations and courage that eventually produces the elation effect. One way of demonstrating elation in the program, and in real life, is a shift from a frustrating experience to one with a large reward. This effect is shown in the graph in Figure 5-2. Using program RAT RACE 3, it is possible to find other sequences of experience that will also produce elation effects.

RAT RACE 3 now contains the three major constructs necessary to describe many research findings in psychology. The readings at the end of this chapter provide many examples of laboratory and real-life situations simulated by RAT RACE 3. Try to simulate the relationship between your own behavior and its consequences, or that of someone else you know. You might be surprised to find some similarity between the results of running this program and life in your world.

APPLICATIONS

The fact that behavior is affected by its consequences is now widely accepted in the behavioral sciences. And the study of reinforcement, at long last, has given psychologists procedures that are effectively changing people's lives. Many behavior modification procedures used in teaching, psychotherapy, social work, personnel management, and child rearing derive from basic research on the effects of reward on behavior. Program RAT RACE illustrates a few basic rules that describe the results of much of that basic research. Obviously, there are many potential applications of these rules. Program RAT RACE was originally developed as an instructional program. In this chapter, I will describe some educational uses of the program. Other applications will be described briefly and then expanded in Chapter 9.

Educational Applications

Informing students that rewards increase the frequency of behaviors and that punishment decreases them comes as no surprise. Therefore, little learning occurs. In order for behavior to change, its consequences must be surprising. The outcomes of many computer simulations of reward are, however, surprising. Program RAT RACE provides animated graphics simulations of many surprising effects of reward on behavior. Let me describe a typical classroom application of the program.

Students are each seated at an Apple II computer with program RAT RACE loaded and ready to use. I instruct the students to give one rat a large reward for running (say twelve to twenty pellets) and the other rat a smaller reward (say three to eight pellets). I then ask them to give fifteen training trials using the same reward conditions. They see, not surprisingly, that the rat receiving the large reward begins to reach the goal box sooner than the one receiving the small reward. At this point, we stop and talk about changing behavior. I point out that in order for behavior to change, the present behavior must be eliminated. Then I ask the class which of their two rats will slow down the soonest if reward is removed. They invariably say that the one trained with the small reward will stop running sooner than the one trained with the large reward. I then instruct them to give ten trials with zero reward. Most students are quite surprised when the large-reward rat runs slower than the small-reward rat. They express doubts and I suggest that they try the same procedure again using two different reward amounts. Of course, they see similar results.

By this time, there typically is chatter among the students about their simulation results. Some students inevitably comment on how cute the simulated rats are. I regain the student's attention and tell them that these results are perfectly consistent with our research results and contemporary knowledge of behavior. Then I ask them why these results occur. It is useful here to refer to such things as expecting the candy machine to dispense chocolates and not receiving the chocolate. We eventually arrive at the notion of frustration and avoidance behavior, and the fact that the amount of frustration depends on the amount of expectation. At this point, I ask students to make other deductions from expectation/frustration theory and to test those deductions using program RAT RACE. If no one develops the idea of depression as a consequence of reward reduction, I suggest it.

I have found program RAT RACE to be a very effective teaching tool. When I finally get around to presenting the formal model on which it is based, the students have already seen many simulated examples of those rules. I suspect that RAT RACE is an effective instructional tool for a fairly simple reason. The student's behavior controls the relationship between the animated rat's behavior and its consequences. And the consequences of some of the students' behavior is surprising. They are surprised at the depression and resistance-to-change simulations that they see demonstrated on the screen. They are surprised when they see that behaviors that are always followed by reward go away faster than those that are only occasionally followed by rewards. What they have learned at this point is that the simple notion "more reward leads to more learning" is inadequate.

I now return to the lecture format and attempt to make a couple of general points. First, there is a general model that describes these exceptions and other phenomena. Second, it is difficult to use the model in one's head. Computer simulation appears not only to be useful but also necessary to an understanding of behavior. The effects of rewards and nonrewards on behavior depends on the individual's prior experience with rewards and nonrewards. It is difficult for us to reason through those effects in our heads. Computer simulation helps us with that difficult task.

Educational applications of program RAT RACE are not restricted to the college or university setting. Since it simply provides animated examples of the effects of rewards and nonrewards on behavior and does not demand that a user understand the model on which it is based, RAT RACE can be used in high-school settings with ease. Many of the outcomes a user encounters in running the program are surprising. At a minimum, the program user will learn not to accept the simple notion that the larger the reward, the stronger the behavior. The illustrations that constitute the output of program RAT RACE can provide the user with a list of exceptions to that rule. He or she will then be in need of a new model to organize his or her knowledge.

Since our economy has become very service oriented, and we are committed to a large number of social programs directed toward long-term goals, many people need better knowledge of human behavior in their professional lives. And they need knowledge that is demonstrably effective, not just the subject matter of imaginative fiction. Program RAT RACE is based on a model of behavior that is consistent with a larger number of research findings than any other model of behavior. In addition, its ideas have been successfully applied in a variety of educational settings such as classrooms and personnel training. Program RAT RACE can be used in many professional training settings—in-service training, seminars, employee training programs, and so on. It can be the foundation of a refresher training course for social workers, teachers, law-enforcement personnel, supervisors of all kinds, managers, ministers—in short, anyone who works with people.

Program RAT RACE can be used as a simulation to answer "what-if" questions when designing programs to help people change their behavior. What would happen, for example, if your child were being rewarded only occasionally for reading, and during a summer visit his or her grandparents gave continuous reward for reading? Program RAT RACE can be used to help you answer that question. And then, what if upon returning home the reward schedule was changed back to an occasional one?

Applications to Computer Games, Operating Systems, and Robotics

The psychological model that RAT RACE 3 is based on has substantial generality. It has been found to describe research results across a wide variety of behaviors and species (including humans). The fact that the program simulates rats running a runway for food rewards is a joint product of my desire to provide students with lifelike simulations and my own years of experience in an animal behavior laboratory. If these programs had been written by an educational psychologist, they might depict a child learning to read for the social approval of a parent. If the programs had been written by a clinical psychologist, they might depict a person learning a variety of social skills in order to obtain dates with someone of the opposite sex. The fact that the psychological model has considerable generality suggests other applications of Artificial Behavior.

AB suggests an entirely new genre of computer games. Current adventure games require the user to type in psychological characteristics of a game character. These traits are than used in conditional branching routines—a persistent character does this, a flighty character does that. The output is then printed to the screen, or a new picture is drawn. In AB games, the characters would be animated on the screen. The game player would control the consequences of behavior—rewards and punishments. The game character's behaviors would change continuously. Some behaviors might be very resistant to change. Other behaviors might change with ease. The games might have specific goals, in which case the player would have to manipulate the relationship between behavior and rewards to produce the pattern of behavior necessary to achieve the goal. The games could be open ended—computer soap operas or interactive fiction. This idea for computer gaming will be expanded in Chapter 9.

The rules governing the development of expectation, frustration, and courage also could be incorporated into software that governs the operation of a computer system (operating systems). In this case, a computer would be able to develop expectations, be frustrated, show elation and depression, and become superstitious. The rules also could be given to robots who would then show more life-like patterns of behavior. Again, these applications of AB will be expanded in Chapter 9.

SUMMARY

If an individual expects to be frustrated and is rewarded, he or she learns courage. The rule governing the acquisition of courage is the same as the rule governing changes in expectation and changes in frustration. Changes in courage are a fraction of the difference between the amount of frustration expected and the amount of courage already learned: $\Delta C = F(E - - C)$. Incorporating courage into our model allows the simulation of the fact that partially rewarded behaviors are extremely resistant to change. RAT RACE 3 also can simulate elation effects and the effect of overlearning on behavior. The addition of courage completes the development of the psychological model to be used for programs later in this book.

Program RAT RACE 3 facilitates students' learning that the simple idea "more reward produces more behavior" is inadequate. By simulating the effects of changes in amount of reward, and 100 percent versus 50 percent schedules of reward, students are primed for the development of alternative ways of conceptualizing the effects of reward on behavior. Artificial Behavior also can be used in operating systems and robotics to facilitate the development of more human-like machines.

ADDITIONAL READINGS

This book is a textbook for college courses entitled Learning or Learning and Motivation. It presents an excellent summary of our knowledge of the effects on behavior of reinforcement and punishment. It contains many excellent examples drawn from day-to-day life.

1. Logan, F. A., *Fundamentals of Learning and Motivation.* (Dubuque, Iowa: Wm. C. Brown Co., 1981).

This paper presents the mathematical model on which the formulas in program RAT RACE are based. It presents the results of scores of computer simulations run to test the fit of the model to existing research findings. This is the definitive paper that should be read by anyone interested in understanding the model of psychological processes on which RAT RACE is based.

2. Daly, H. B., and Daly, J. T., "A Mathematical Model of Reward and Aversive Nonreward: Its Application in Over 30 Appetitive Learning Situations," *Journal of Experimental Psychology,* 1983, *111,* 441–80.

The following paper reviews the theory on which RAT RACE is based and then discusses its relevance to psychotherapeutic treatment of depression, acquired fears, assertiveness training, and other psychological interventions.

3. Nation, J. R., and Woods, D. J., "Persistence: The Role of Partial Reinforcement in Psychotherapy," *Journal of Experimental Psychology: General,* 1980, *109,* 175–207.

6

SPONTANEITY

Programs
RAT 1
and PIGEON 1

The behavior of a rat running down a runway, simulated in program RAT RACE, is a simplified laboratory model for studying the effects of reward and nonreward on behavior. Use of the computer simulation illustrates that rewards and nonrewards are important determiners of such psychological processes as expectations, frustration, courage, elation, depression, persistence, and resistance to change. Incorporation of the knowledge simulated by program RAT RACE into such things as computer games and operating systems was suggested at the end of Chapter 5. RAT RACE, however, contains one characteristic that impedes direct incorporation of its algorithms into other applications software.

The running response in program RAT RACE cannot occur until the computer places the rat in the start box of the runway and the program user pushes the S key to open the start-box door. The suggestions for computer games and operating systems in Chapter 5 require environments in which behavior is freely available. There are other procedures in the study of the effects of rewards on behavior that more realistically simulate a free environment. B. F. Skinner described such procedures in his 1938 book, *The Behavior of Organisms*. In one such procedure, a hungry rat is placed into a chamber containing a small light, a tray for food delivery, and a lever protruding from a wall. In another procedure, a hungry pigeon is placed into a chamber containing a light, a food tray, and a circular disk mounted on the wall. In the first procedure, the rat's frequency of lever pressing can be modified by reward and in the second the pigeon's frequency of disk pecking can be modified by rewards. These two experimental arrangements are now commonly referred to as Skinner Boxes.

This chapter will present simulations of these two Skinner Boxes. Chapter 7 will illustrate a more complex Skinner Box containing two environmental objects to manipulate (a lever to press and a chain to pull), each with its own schedule of reward. These Skinner Box simulations will allow us to free the organism to respond whenever he "feels like it," and then to develop simulations of an organism with more than one behavior and more than one schedule of reward. The more complex simulations will facilitate the use of many of our psychological principles in more interesting ways. In addition, the simulation in Chapter 7 will allow us to begin looking at how an individual chooses between alternative things to do in his world. The simple Skinner Box simulations in this chapter will set the stage for our examination of these more complex issues.

SIMULATING FREELY OCCURRING BEHAVIOR

While many behaviors appear to arise spontaneously (some are instinctual, some are acquired by observing the behavior of other people, some are shaped by reinforcement, some are instructed, etc.), their rate of subsequent occurrence is affected by their consequences. Programs RAT 1 and PIGEON 1 begin by drawing a picture of a rat or pigeon in a Skinner Box. If you are patient enough, the rat eventually will press the lever, or the pigeon will peck the disk, for no apparent reason. (This is similar to the experience you would have if you were sitting in front of a Skinner Box in an animal behavior laboratory.) If that response is not followed by food, the behavior will be even less likely to occur in the future. If the behavior is followed by reward, the animal will begin to develop an expectation that lever pressing or disk pecking is followed by food, and will be more likely to press the lever or peck the disk in the future. In these two simulations, just as in real Skinner Boxes, the reason for the initial behavior is unknown; however, its rate of future occurrence is governed by its consequences.

In programs PIGEON 1 and RAT 1, just as in program RAT RACE, food reward increases the expectation of reward. That expectation produces an increase in running speed in RAT RACE, but in these programs it produces an increase in the rate of lever pressing or disk pecking. While nonreward trivially reduces expectations of reward, once an expectation of reward develops, nonreward is a violation of the animal's expectation and produces frustration, which interferes with the ongoing lever pressing or disk pecking. Rewards that are obtained when frustration is expected produce courage. In these situations, the rat or pigeon acquires courage to press the lever or peck the disk even when it is uncertain about the consequences. These two programs use the same psychological constructs and computation algorithms as program RAT RACE; however, the simulated organisms are now free to respond whenever they feel like it.

DESCRIPTION OF PROGRAM RAT 1

Program RAT 1 is written in a modular format. Lines 100 through 490 constitute the main control program. Lines 500 through 610 are the animation routine for the rat lever-press behavior. Lines 700 through 990 are the calculation routine for the psychological processes. Lines 1000 through 1090 deliver the food rewards and animate the food consumption by the rat. Lines 3000 through 3250 draw the initial graphics on the screen. The program was explicitly designed in this modular form so that some of its parts can be readily used in other Artificial Behavior programs. The control program (lines 100 through 490) and the calculation of the psychological processes (lines 700 through 990) will be used in program PIGEON 1 exactly as they are in program RAT 1. All that must be done is a drawing of a pigeon must be substituted for that of a rat beginning at line 3000, animate disk pecking must occur instead of lever pressing at lines 500 through 610, and grain must be the reward instead of food pellets beginning at line 1000. The control program and the psychological calculations can remain the same for these two programs and many other potential AB programs.

What follows is a detailed description of program RAT 1. Line 110 calls a subroutine beginning at line 3000. This subroutine draws a rat in a Skinner Box and then returns control to line 120. Line 120 sets two variables, T1 and T4, equal to 0.05. These variables are exactly as used in program RAT RACE. T1 is the value of the expectation of reward and T4 is the sum of expectation of reward (T1), minus expectations of frustration (T2), plus courage (T3). The variables and formulas used in the psychological calculations for program RAT 1 are exactly the same as those used in program RAT RACE. The initial value of 0.05 for T1 and T4 means that the rat has some very small expectation of reward for lever pressing at the outset and hence will have some initial low probability of lever-press behavior. This is the source of the initial lever press in the program. Line 0150 sets five other variables equal to 0. Each of these will be explained as we encounter them in the program.

Each time it is executed, line 160 increments the variable PL by 1. This variable will be used to subscript the function RND to generate a random number. If the function RND does not have a new subscript each time it is executed in APPLESOFT BASIC, it will return the same random number over and over again. Line 0180 clears the memory location used for storing the results of a keyboard strobe. A keypress is used in this program to allow the program user to reward the rat. Line 200 checks the keyboard strobe (PEEK -16384) to see if the R key has been struck. If the user has depressed the R key, it means he or she wants the next lever press to be followed by food. The results of the keyboard strobe are assigned to the variable AA. If the letter R has been struck, the number 210 has been stored at memory location -16384. If AA is equal to 210, a new variable R is set equal to 1. When R is 0, the next lever press will not be followed by food; when R is 1, it will be followed by a food reward.

Line 205 generates a random number between 0 and 100 and assigns it to the variable RN. Line 210 converts the variable T4 (total response strength from the psychological model) to an integer value by multiplying it times 100 and eliminating any remaining decimal fraction. This new value is assigned to the variable T5. Line 215 checks the keyboard strobe again to see if the program user has hit the R key. Line 220 takes the reciprocal of T4 and multiplies it times 30 and assigns the product to the variable BB. The larger the response strength indicated by T4, the smaller the value of BB. Line 230 checks the keyboard strobe again. Line 240 sets up a counting loop from 1 to BB. The lower the response strength (T4), the larger the value of BB, and therefore the longer it will take to count the loop. This loop helps time the rate of occurrence of lever-pressing behavior. The lower the value of T4, the longer the count and hence the longer the time between lever presses. The keyboard strobe is checked during each execution of the loop in line 240. Line 250 assigns R the value of 1 if the user has hit the R key or branches to line 2900, which stops the program if the user has hit the S key. Line 0260 sends program control to line 500 if RN has a value of less than T5. This means that if the random number (RN) is less than the integer value for response strength (T5), a lever press will be executed. Line 270 sends program control back to line 200 if the R key has been pressed. This repeats the random number generating until RN is less than T5 and a lever press occurs. Lines 280 through 300 read the keyboard strobe again and perform the appropriate branching, depending on its results. Line 310 returns control to 200 if the R key has been depressed and to line 160 if it has not been depressed.

Lines 500 through 610 perform the lever-press animation. If the R key has been pressed, line 700 calls a subroutine at lines 1000 through 1090 that dispenses a food pellet and animates the consumption of the food pellet. Control is then returned to line 750. Lines 750 through 990 carry out the calculations. These lines are exactly the same as lines 3000 through 3490 of RAT RACE 3 in the preceding chapter. The psychological model used to calculate the probability of a lever press is the same one used to calculate running speed in RAT RACE. In the present program, all of the REMarks have been removed,

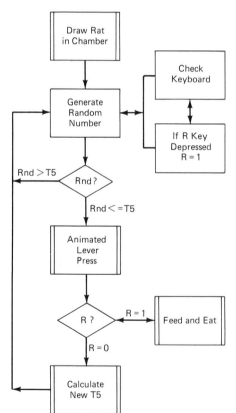

Figure 6-1. Flow chart of program RAT 1. First, the graphics are drawn on the screen. Then the computer generates a random number and checks to see if the user has depressed the R key. The random number is then compared to the response strength (T5). If the random number is greater than T5, a new random number is generated. If it is smaller than T5, the lever-press animation occurs. Following a lever press, food is delivered and eaten if R = 1. Then a new value of T5 is calculated based on the occurrence or nonoccurrence of food.

but the calculations are identical. This calculation routine results in a new value for T4, prints it at the bottom of the screen, and returns control to the main program (line 150). Figure 6-1 is a flowchart of program RAT 1.

PROGRAM LISTING

RAT 1

```
0100   REM   MAIN PROGRAM
0110   GOSUB 3000
0120   T1 = .05: T4 = .05
0150   R = 0:RN = 0:AA = 0:S = 0:PL = 0:X = FRE (0)
0160   PL = PL + 1
0180   POKE - 16368,0
0190   REM   GENERATE RANDOM #
0200   AA = PEEK (-16384):IF AA = 210 THEN R = 1
0205   RN = INT (100 * RND (PL))
0210   T5 = INT (100 * T4)
0215   AA = PEEK (-16384):IF AA = 210 THEN R = 1
0220   BB = 30 * (1/T4)
0230   AA = PEEK (-16384)
0240   FOR K = 1 TO BB:AA = PEEK (-16384):NEXT K
0250   IF AA = 210 THEN R = 1:IF AA = 211 THEN GOTO 2900
0260   IF RN < = T5 THEN GOTO 500
0270   IF R = 1 THEN GOTO 200
0280   AA = PEEK (-16384)
0290   IF AA = 210 THEN R = 1
0300   IF AA = 211 THEN GOTO 2900
0310   IF R = 1 THEN GOTO 200
0320   IF R = 0 THEN GOTO 160
0490   REM   ANIMATES BAR PRESS
0500   HCOLOR = 0:HPLOT 52,125 TO 74,125 TO 52,126 TO 74,126
       TO 52,127 TO 74,127 TO 52,128 TO 75,128 TO 52,129 TO
       75,129
0510   HCOLOR=2:HPLOT 54,125 TO 64,132 TO 54,126 TO 64,133 TO
       54,127 TO 64,134
0520   HPLOT 62,134 TO 69,134 TO 61,135 TO 61,135 TO 69,135 TO
       61,136 TO 68,136 TO 60,137 TO 66,137:HPLOT 65,129 TO 70,
       129 TO 66,128 TO 70,128
0530   HCOLOR = 0:HPLOT 85,126 TO 71,131 TO 85,127 TO 71,132 TO
       85,128:HCOLOR=3:HPLOT 85,126 TO 70,133 TO 85,127 TO 70,
       134 TO 85,128 TO 70,134 TO 85,129
0540   REM   SOUND EFFECT
0550   S=(-16336):FOR BEEP = 1 TO 10:SOUND = PEEK (S):NEXT BEEP
0560   REM   CONTINUE ANIMATION
0570   FOR I = 1 TO 100:NEXT I
0580   HCOLOR=0:HPLOT 54,125 TO 64,132 TO 54,126 TO 64,133 TO
       54,127 TO 64,134:HCOLOR =2:HPLOT 54,125 TO 65,128 TO
       54,126 TO 65,129 TO 54,127 TO 66,127
```

```
0590   HCOLOR=0:HPLOT 60,134 TO 70,134 TO 70,135 TO 60,135 TO
       60,136 TO 70,136 TO 70,137 TO 60,137:HCOLOR =2:HPLOT 71,
       129 TO 63,129 TO 64,128 TO 71,128 TO 72,127 TO 65,127 TO
       66,126 TO 72,126 TO 68,125 TO 66,125
0600   HPLOT 66,134 TO 71,134 TO 71,135 TO 68,135:HCOLOR=0:HPLOT
       85,126 TO 70,133 TO 85,127 TO 70,134 TO 85,129:HCOLOR=3:
       HPLOT 85,126 TO 71,131 TO 85,127 TO 71,132 TO 85,128
0610   HPLOT 75,130 TO 85,130:HCOLOR=0:HPLOT 80,131 TO 95,131
0700   IF R = 1 THEN GOSUB 1000
0750   REM   CALCULATION SUBROUTINE
0760   IF R = 0 THEN 0 = .00
0770   IF R = 1 THEN 0 = 1.00
0780   IF 0 < T1 THEN GOTO 850
0790   E1 = .05 * (0 - T1)
0800   IF T2 < = 0 THEN GOTO 910
0810   E2 = .01 * (0 - T2)
0820   E3 = .05 * (T2 - T3)
0840   GOTO 910
0850   OX = ABS (2 * (0 - T1))
0860   E2 = .05 * (OX - T2)
0870   IF T1 < 0 THEN GOTO 910
0880   E1 = .01 * (0 - T1)
0890   IF E2 < = 0 THEN GOTO 910
0900   E3 = .01 * (0 - T3)
0910   T1 = (T1 + E1)
0920   T2 = (T2 + E2)
0930   T3 = (T3 + E3)
0940   T4 = (T4 + (E1 - (E2/2) + E3))
0950   PRINT:PRINT:PRINT "EXPECTATION = "T4
0960   GOTO 150
0990   REM   END CALCULATIONS
1000   REM   DISPENSE FOOD
1010   REM      AND EAT
1020   S = (-16336):FOR BEEP = 1 TO 4:SOUND = PEEK (S):NEXT BEEP
1030   HCOLOR=3:HPLOT 61,114
1040   BF=INT (100 * T4):BG=500/BF:FOR J = 1 TO BF:NEXT J
1050   HCOLOR=3:HPLOT 63,114 TO 67,114:HPLOT 64,115 TO 65,115:
       HCOLOR=0:HPLOT 64,117 TO 66,117:HPLOT 65,118 TO 67,118:
       HPLOT 66,119 TO 69,119:HPLOT
1060   HCOLOR = 0:HPLOT 63,114 TO 67,114:HPLOT 64,115 TO 65,115:
       HCOLOR=3:HPLOT 64,117 TO 66,117:HPLOT 65,118 TO 67,118:
       HPLOT 66,119 TO 69,119
1090   RETURN
2900   TEXT:HOME:END
3000   REM   MAIN DRAWING
3010   REM      ROUTINE
3020   POKE 230,32:CALL 62450:HGR:HCOLOR=3
3030   REM   OUTLINES BOX
3040   HPLOT 47,160 TO 76,88 TO 76,10:HPLOT 76,88 TO 250,88
3050   REM   DRAWS RAT
3060   HPLOT 118,102 TO 131,102:HPLOT 110,103 TO 138,103:HPLOT
       103,104 TO 141,104:HPLOT 101,105 TO 143,105:HPLOT 97,106
       TO 144,106:HPLOT 78,106 TO 84,106
3070   HPLOT 75,107 TO 145,107:HPLOT 74,108 TO 146,108:HPLOT
       73,109 TO 147,109:HPLOT 72,110 TO 148,110:HPLOT 71,111 TO
```

```
      150,111:HPLOT 70,112 TO 151,112
3080  HPLOT 69,113 TO 151,113:HPLOT 68,114 TO 153,114:HPLOT
      67,115 TO 154,115:HPLOT 66,116 TO 155,116:HPLOT 65,117
      TO 157,117:HPLOT 64,118 TO 159,118
3090  HPLOT 65,119 TO 77,119:HPLOT 82,119 TO 161,119:HPLOT
      67,120 TO 75,120:HPLOT 83,120 TO 164,120:HPLOT 82,121 TO
      171,121:HPLOT 82,122 TO 194,122
3100  HPLOT 81,123 TO 197,123:HPLOT 80,124 TO 83,124:HPLOT
      85,124 TO 198,124:HPLOT 79,125 TO 82,125:HPLOT 85,125 TO
      140,125:HPLOT 151,125 TO 200,125
3110  HPLOT 78,126 TO 81,126:HPLOT 85,126 TO 136,126:HPLOT
      193,126 TO 201,126:HPLOT 77,127 TO 78,127:HPLOT 89,127 TO
      133,127:HPLOT 197,127 TO 201,127
3120  HPLOT 93,128 TO 101,128:HPLOT 115,128 TO 125,128:HPLOT
      198,128 TO 201,128:HPLOT 129,128 TO 133,128:HPLOT 114,
      129 TO 122,129:HPLOT 128,129 TO 132,129
3130  HPLOT 199,129 TO 202,129:HPLOT 114,130 TO 121,130:HPLOT
      125,130 TO 133,130:HPLOT 200,130 TO 203,130:HPLOT 112,
      131 TO 118,131:HPLOT 123,131 TO 132,131
3140  HPLOT 200,131 TO 203,131:HPLOT 112,132 TO 115,132:HPLOT
      122,132 TO 128,132:HPLOT 201,132 TO 203,132:HPLOT
      123,133 TO 125,133:HPLOT 201,133 TO 185,144
3150  HPLOT 202,133 TO 190,140:HCOLOR=0:HPLOT 73,113 TO
      74,113:HCOLOR=3:HPLOT 73,108 TO 73,105:HPLOT 74,105 TO
      74,108:HPLOT 75,106 TO 75,108
3160  REM   END RAT
3170  REM   DRAWS LEVER
3180  HCOLOR=2:HPLOT 54,125 TO 65,128:HPLOT 54,126 TO 65,129:
      HPLOT 54,127 TO 66,127
3190  HPLOT 66,125 TO 68,125:HPLOT 66,126 TO 72,126:HPLOT
      65,127 TO 72,127:HPLOT 64,128 TO 71,128:HPLOT 63,129 TO
      71,129:HPLOT 63,130 TO 70,130:HPLOT 63,131 TO 70,131:
      HPLOT 62,132 TO 70,132
3200  HPLOT 62,133 TO 70,133:HPLOT 66,134 TO 71,134:HPLOT 68,
      135 TO 71,135
3210  REM   DRAWS LEFT PAW
3220  HCOLOR=3:HPLOT 91,126 TO 72,131:HPLOT 92,126 TO 71,132:
      HPLOT 93,126 TO 71,132:HPLOT 94,126 TO 71,132
3230  HPLOT 88,127 TO 82,127:HPLOT 89,128 TO 84,128:HPLOT
      89,129 TO 80,129:HPLOT 88,130 TO 75,130:HPLOT 85,131 TO
      75,131:HPLOT 79,132 TO 70,132
3240  HPLOT 61,110 TO 60,110 TO 57,117 TO 61,117:HPLOT 62,
      116 TO 63,115 TO 63,112 TO 62,111
3250  RETURN
```

Program PIGEON 1 is functionally identical to program RAT 1. Instead of a rat that lever presses for food pellets, PIGEON 1 simulates a pigeon pecking a disk for grain. Animation of the pigeon disk-pecking response requires that the entire head and neck of the pigeon move forward and back. Animation of the feeding response requires that the head and neck move down to the grain dispenser and back up. Since the parts of the body to be animated are so much larger than the rat forearm, the graphics animation routines of PIGEON 1 are somewhat larger (and slower) than those of RAT 1.

PROGRAM LISTING

PIGEON 1


```
0100
------
------
                (SAME AS RAT 1)
------
------
0320


0500    REM   ANIMATES PECK
0510    HCOLOR = 3:HPLOT 135,56 TO 135,55 TO 136,55 TO 137,54
        TO 135,54 TO 135,53 TO 138,53:HPLOT 136,43 TO 137,43
        TO 137,44 TO 136,44
0520    HCOLOR=3:HPLOT 136,52 TO 140,52:HPLOT 137,51 TO 142,51
        TO 143,50 TO 138,50 TO 139,49 TO 145,49:HPLOT 147,48 TO
        140,48 TO 148,47 TO 158,47 TO 158,46 TO 148,46
0530    HCOLOR=0:HPLOT 112.52 TO 114,52 TO 113,51 TO 115,51 TO
        115,50 TO 118,50 TO 119,49 TO 116,49 TO 118,48 TO 121,48
        TO 120,47 TO 124,47:HPLOT 122,46 TO 126,46
0540    HCOLOR=3:HPLOT 147,45 TO 157,45:HPLOT 146,44 TO 155,44
        TO 154,43 TO 145,43:HPLOT 143,42 TO 153,42 TO 152,41
        TO 143,41 TO 142,40 TO 151,40 TO 150,39 TO 141,39
0550    HCOLOR=0:HPLOT 124,45 TO 129,45:HPLOT 126,44 TO 131,44
        TO 132,43 TO 126,43 TO 127,42 TO 133,42 TO 134,41 TO
        129,41 TO 129,40 TO 135,40:HPLOT 132,39 TO 137,39
0560    HCOLOR=0:HPLOT 144,43 TO 145,43 TO 145,44 TO 144,44
0600    S = (-16336): FOR BEEP = 1 TO 10:SOUND = PEEK (S):
        NEXT BEEP
0610    FOR X = 1 TO 100:NEXT X
0620    HCOLOR=0:HPLOT 141,39 TO 151,39 TO 152,40 TO 142,40 TO
        143,41 TO 153,41:HCOLOR=3:HPLOT 132,39 TO 140,39 TO
        141,40 TO 130,40 TO 129,41 TO 142,41
0630    HCOLOR=0:HPLOT 144,42 TO 154,42 TO 155,43 TO 145,53 TO
        146,44 TO 156,44 TO 157,45 TO 147,45:HCOLOR=3:HPLOT 128,42
        TO 143,42 TO 144,43 TO 127,43 TO 126,44 TO 145,44 TO
        146,45 TO 124,45
0640    HCOLOR=0:HPLOT 148,46 TO 158,46 TO 158,47 TO 148,47:
        HPLOT 140,48 TO 150,48:HCOLOR=3:HPLOT 122,46 TO 147,46
        TO 147,47 TO 120,47:HPLOT 118,48 TO 139,48
0650    HCOLOR=0:HPLOT 139,49 TO 147,49:HPLOT 138,50 TO 145,50:
        HPLOT 137,51 TO 143,51:HCOLOR=3:HPLOT 117,49 TO 138,49
        TO 137,50 TO 116,50:HPLOT 114,51 TO 136,51
0660    HCOLOR=3:HPLOT 113,52 TO 135,52 TO 134,53 TO 110,53:
        HCOLOR=0:HPLOT 136,52 TO 141,52:HPLOT 135,53 TO 140,53:
        HPLOT 135,54 TO 138,54
0670    HPLOT 135,55 TO 137,55 TO 137,56:HPLOT 136,43 TO 137,43
        TO 137,44 TO 136,44:HCOLOR=3
```

```
0700
----
----            (SAME AS RAT 1)

----
----
0990


1000    REM   DISPENSE FOOD
1010    REM     AND EAT
1020    HCOLOR=3:GOSUB 1500
1030    S=(-16336):FOR BEEP = 1 TO 6:SOUND = PEEK (S):
        NEXT BEEP
1040    HCOLOR = 0:GOSUB 1600
1050    HCOLOR = 3:GOSUB 1700
1060    FOR X = 1 TO 200:NEXT X
1070    HCOLOR = 0:GOSUB 1500
1080    HCOLOR = 0:GOSUB 1700
1090    HCOLOR = 3:GOSUB 1800
1100    HCOLOR = 0:HPLOT 136,43 TO 137,43 TO 137,44 TO 136,44:
        HCOLOR = 3
1110    HPLOT 148,80 TO 148,100 TO 174,107 TO 174,87 TO 148,80
1200    RETURN
1500    REM   FOOD SUBROUTINE
1510    HPLOT 161,99 TO 150,99 TO 151,100 TO 164,100 TO 165,101
        TO 154,101:HPLOT 159,102 TO 168,102:HPLOT 163,103 TO
        170,103 TO 171,104 TO 166,104
1550    RETURN
1600    REM   HEAD UP SUBROUTINE
1610    HPLOT 131,39 TO 142,39 TO 143,40 TO 129,40 TO 128,41 TO
        145,41 TO 144,42 TO 127,42 TO 126,43 TO 149,43 TO 150,44
        TO 125,44:HPLOT 123,45 TO 151, 45 TO 151,46 TO
        121,46
1620    HPLOT 119,47 TO 148,47:HPLOT 117,48 TO 140,48 TO 139,49
        TO 116,49 TO 115,50 TO 138,50 TO 137,51 TO 113,51 TO
        112,52 TO 136,52 TO 135,53 TO 109,53 TO 108,54 TO 135,54
1630    HPLOT 106,55 TO 135,55 TO 135,56 TO 107,56:HPLOT
        103,57 TO 135,57 TO 134,58 TO 104,58:HPLOT 107,59 TO
        134,59 TO 135,60 TO 109,60:HPLOT 113,61 TO 136,61 TO
        136,62 TO 117,62
1640    HPLOT 119,63 TO 137,63 TO 137,64 TO 121,64:HPLOT 124,65 TO
        138,65 TO 138,66 TO 127,66:HPLOT 131,67 TO 138,67 TO
        138,68 TO 134,68:HPLOT 137,69 TO 138,69
1690    RETURN
1700    REM   HEAD DOWN SUBROUTINE
1710    HPLOT 139,70 TO 139,72 TO 142,72:HPLOT 139,73 TO 144,73
        TO 146,74 TO 139,74 TO 139,75 TO 148,75:HPLOT 152,76 TO
        138,76 TO 138,77 TO 155,77 TO 156,78 TO 138,78
1720    HPLOT 138,79 TO 156,79 TO 157,80 TO 137,80 TO 136,81 TO
        158,82 TO 136,82 TO 135,83 TO 159,83 TO 159,84 TO 134,84
        TO 134,85 TO 160,85 TO 160,86 TO 133,86
1730    HPLOT 132,87 TO 159,87 TO 159,88 TO 131,88:HPLOT 146,89
```

```
          TO 159,89 TO 159,90 TO 150,90:HPLOT 153,91 TO 158,91:
          HPLOT 158,96 TO 158,92 TO 157,92 TO 157,94:HPLOT 155,95
          TO 155,92 TO 154,92
1790      RETURN
1800      REM   HEAD UP SUBROUTINE
1810      HPLOT 138,69 TO 137,69:HPLOT 134,68 TO 138,68 TO 138,67
          TO 131,67:HPLOT 127,66 TO 138,66 TO 138,65 TO 124,65:
          HPLOT 121,64 TO 137,64 TO 137,63 TO 119,63
1820      HPLOT 117,62 TO 136,62 TO 136,61 TO 113,61:HPLOT 109,60
          TO 135,60 TO 134,59 TO 107,59:HPLOT 104,58 TO 134,58 TO
          134,57 TO 104,57:HPLOT 108,56 TO 134,56 TO 134,55 TO
          107,55
1830      HPLOT 134,54 TO 109,54 TO 110,53 TO 134,53 TO 135,52 TO
          113,52 TO 114,51 TO 136,51 TO 137,50 TO 116,50 TO 117,49
          TO 138,49 TO 139,48 TO 118,48:HPLOT 147,47 TO 120,47
1840      HPLOT 122,46 TO 147,46 TO 146,45 TO 124,45:HPLOT 126,44
          TO 145,44 TO 144,43 TO 127,43 TO 128,42 TO 143,42 TO
          142,41 TO 129,41 TO 130,40 TO 142,40 TO 141,39 TO 132,39
1850      RETURN
2900      TEXT:HOME:END
3000      REM   MAIN DRAWING
3010      REM   ROUTINE
3020      POKE 230,32:CALL 62450:HGR:HCOLOR=3
3030      HPLOT 89,98 TO 113,98:HPLOT 115,97 TO 84,97:HPLOT 81,96
          TO 118,96 TO 119,95 TO 78,95:HPLOT 68,94 TO 121,94 TO
          122,93 TO 65,93
3040      HPLOT 63,92 TO 124,92 TO 125,91 TO 61,91 TO 60,90 TO
          126,90:HPLOT 128,89 TO 58,89:HPLOT 56,88 TO 130,88 TO
          131,87 TO 55,87 TO 54,86 TO 132,86
3050      HPLOT 133,85 TO 53,85 TO 52,84 TO 133,84 TO 134,83 TO
          51,83 TO 50,82 TO 135,82 TO 135,81 TO 49,81 TO 48,80 TO
          136,80 TO 137,79 TO 48,79
3060      HPLOT 48,78 TO 137,78 TO 137,77 TO 49,77:HPLOT 51,76 TO
          137,76 TO 138,75 TO 53,75:HPLOT 59,74 TO 138,74 TO 138,73
          TO 63,73 TO 62,72 TO 138,72 TO 138,71 TO 61,71
3070      HPLOT 64,70 TO 138,70 TO 138,69 TO 65,69 TO 66,68 TO
          138,68 TO 138,67 TO 67,67:HPLOT 73,66 TO 138,66 TO 138,65
          TO 73,65
3080      HPLOT 74,64 TO 137,64 TO 137,63 TO 93,63 TO 94,62 TO
          136,62 TO 136,61 TO 98,61 TO 99,60 TO 135,60
3090      HPLOT 100,59 TO 134,59 TO 134,58 TO 101,58:HPLOT 104,57
          TO 134,57 TO 134,56 TO 108,56 TO 107,55 TO 134,55 TO
          134,54 TO 109,54 TO 110,53 TO 134,53
3100      HPLOT 113,52 TO 135,52 TO 136,51 TO 114,51 TO 116,50 TO
          137,50 TO 138,49 TO 117,49 TO 118,48 TO 139,48:HPLOT
          120,47 TO 147,47 TO 147,46 TO 122,46
3110      HPLOT 124,45 TO 146,45 TO 145,44 TO 126,44 TO 127,43 TO
          144,43 TO 143,42 TO 128,42 TO 129,41 TO 142,41 TO 141,40
          TO 130,40
3120      HPLOT 132,39 TO 140,39:HCOLOR=0:HPLOT 136,43 TO 137,43 TO
          137,44 TO 136,44:HCOLOR=2:HPLOT 63,74 TO 106,92:HCOLOR=3
3130      HPLOT 103,99 TO 103,108 TO 102,108 TO 102,99:HPLOT 102,
          108 TO 109,108 TO 109,109 TO 102,109:HPLOT 108,99 TO
          108,111 TO 109,111 TO 109,99
```

```
3140   HPLOT 109,111 TO 116,111:HPLOT 0,15 TO 95,15 TO 99,90:
       HPLOT 0,95 TO 95,95:HPLOT 95,15 TO 220,35:HPLOT 95,95 TO
       220,130
3150   HPLOT 158,48 TO 164,48 TO 164,49 TO 158,49:HPLOT 159,47
       TO 163,47 TO 162,46 TO 160,46:HPLOT 161,45
3160   HPLOT 159,50 TO 163,50 TO 162,51 TO 160,51 TO 161,52
3170   HPLOT 148,80 TO 148,100 TO 174,107 TO 174,87 TO 148,80
3180   RETURN
```

USING RAT 1 AND PIGEON 1

When program RAT 1 or program PIGEON 1 have been typed into your computer and stored on the disk or tape, they can be used by typing in "RUN RAT 1" or "RUN PIGEON 1". When either program is RUN, it will begin by drawing the animal in its respective Skinner Box. Now, if you simply watch and wait, the rat eventually will press the lever (program PIGEON 1 is, of course, analogous to the description of program RAT 1). The rate of lever pressing in the absence of food rewards is very slow. You may in fact become impatient waiting the two or three minutes it sometimes takes before the rat presses the lever. This wait can be much longer in the laboratory with a real animal, or in real life when you must wait for someone to perform a behavior before you can reward it. If you depress the R key while the program is running, the next lever

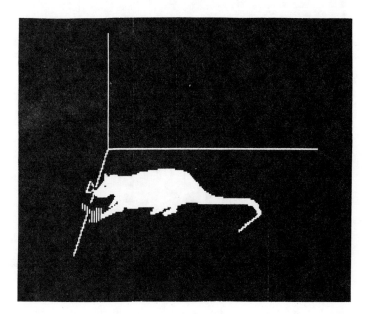

Figure 6-2.   Illustration of the rat in program RAT 1 pressing the lever in the Skinner Box.

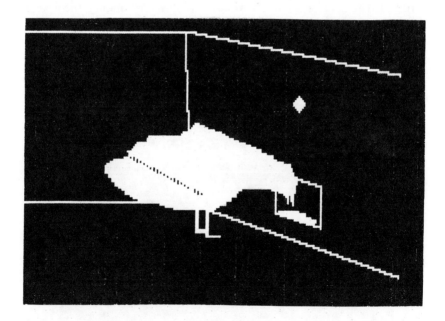

Figure 6-3. Illustrations from program PIGEON 1. In the top picture, the pigeon is pecking the lighted disk in the Skinner Box. In the bottom picture, the pigeon is eating from the grain hopper.

press will be followed immediately by a food reward. Food pellets are delivered into the food tray and the rat eats them before returning to lever pressing.

The rat lever-press response continues to be modified by rewards or nonrewards in the same way running speed was modified in RAT RACE. Now, however, the impression is of real live action. If you don't reward the behavior, it slowly will go away. If you only reward the behavior intermittently, you will discover that the behavior will occur at a high rate and will be very resistant to change. In fact, intermittent reward will raise the level of expectation printed at the bottom of the screen to values of 1.40 and 1.50 quite rapidly. However, remember that our maximum level of expectation was set at 1.00, or unity, in line 770 of the program. The value of O, obtained reward, which sets the limit on expectation, is 1.00. However, recall from our discussion in Chapter 5 that the limit on behavior is expectation, minus frustration, plus courage. The larger the frustration, the greater the amount of courage that is learned if frustration is expected and reward occurs. Program RAT 1 demonstrates the ease with which intermittent rewards produce behaviors that exceed the limit imposed by the reward magnitude. Anyone who has ever worked with rats or pigeons in Skinner Boxes, or who has studied human behavior for that matter, will tell you that is exactly what happens.

The programs in this chapter provide you with much more lively examples of all the psychological principles covered in Chapters 3 through 5. These programs differ from RAT RACE in that the rats or pigeons are now free to lever press or disk peck whenever they want to rather than waiting for the program user to provide the opportunity. The lever-press responses appear to occur spontaneously.

Notice that both of these programs use the same main control routine (lines 100 through 490) and the same calculational routines for determining the effects of rewards and nonrewards on behavior (lines 700 through 990). All the rest of the lines are graphics and animation. It is now very easy for you to substitute any individual engaging in any behavior to create your own Artificial Behavior programs. Use the control program and the calculational subroutine to have a dog learn to fetch sticks for dog biscuit rewards, a fly learn to move toward open food, a child learn to read for social approval, or a knight learn to slay dragons to win a princess. Many excellent utilities exist for the Apple to allow you to easily create graphics drawings and animate them. Most of these can be used with the Artificial Behavior utilities contained in programs RAT 1 and PIGEON 1 to create your own Artificial Behavior programs.

SUMMARY

Application of the ideas developed in Chapters 3 through 5 to computer games and computer operating systems is difficult because program RAT RACE requires the user to open the runway start box door in order to make the running response available to the rat. Many applications of the ideas of learned expectations, frustration, courage, depression, elation, and resistance to change require a freely behaving individual. Fortunately, researchers in psychology also have been interested in the effects of rewards and nonrewards on spontaneously occurring behavior. The well-known Skinner Box procedures were designed to study spontaneously occurring behavior. Program RAT 1 simulates the effects of reward and nonreward on the lever-press behavior of a rat in a Skinner Box, and program PIGEON 1 simulates a similar procedure where a pigeon pecks a disk. The program starts out with a very low level of spontaneously occurring behavior and allows the user to reward or not reward the animal. Rate of behavior changes according to the same rules developed to simulate running speed in RAT RACE. The control routine and psychological calculations routine of programs RAT 1 and PIGEON 1 can be used as utilities to create a wide variety of Artificial Behavior programs.

ADDITIONAL READINGS

1. Skinner, B. F., *The Behavior of Organisms* (New York: Appleton-Century-Crofts, Inc., 1938).
2. Holland, J. G., and Skinner, B. F., *The Analysis of Behavior* (New York: McGraw-Hill Book Company, 1961).

7

CHOICE, FREEDOM

Program
RAT 2

Numerous research psychologists have advocated extending our conclusions about rat lever pressing to human behavior. In *Walden Two* (1948), B. F. Skinner describes a fictional utopian society built entirely on the assumption that human behavior is a function of its consequences. In *Science and Human Behavior* (1953), *Verbal Behavior* (1957), and *Beyond Freedom and Dignity* (1971), Skinner continues his public advocacy of a science of human behavior based on principles of reinforcement. Yet these ideas have encountered substantial criticism. Perhaps the most frequently voiced concern is that what we know from studying behavior in Skinner Boxes is much too simplistic to account for all the subtleties of human behavior. As you see in programs RAT 1 and PIGEON 1, the Skinner Box environment is quite barren. There are only two things for the rat to do—press the lever and eat.

Rats typically are thought of as less complex than humans, and critics see human life as much more complicated than what's encountered in a Skinner Box. At any one time, there are dozens of environmental objects we can operate on and numerous other people to interact with. The process of weighing and choosing among all of the things we can do is crucial in our daily lives, and it is unclear how research in Skinner Boxes addresses these complex processes. One of the most crucial concepts critics point to is choice. Few people argue with the idea that the laws of reinforcement may indeed govern the behavior of a rat in a Skinner Box. A human in a highly varied world, and with minimal political constraints, is free to make choices about what to do and why he or she chooses to do the particular things he does. It is unclear how Skinner Box research informs us about these more complex human situations.

Psychologists have responded to these criticisms in two important ways. One approach has been to apply the principles of reinforcement to human behavior whenever the opportunity arises. That effort has enjoyed considerable success and has produced an approach to psychological interventions in education, therapy, and management that is referred to as behavior modification. A second response to the criticism that our research is too simplistic has been to build more complex Skinner Boxes. This chapter will present a simulation of one of these more complex Skinner Box procedures.

One modification of the Skinner Box involves adding a second object for the rat to manipulate. The simplest example in the laboratory is the addition of a ring that hangs by a chain from the top of the Skinner Box. The ring can be pulled to operate a microswitch. The experimenter can provide rewards for chain pulling and rewards for lever pressing. In the laboratory, an arrangement where two or more behaviors are simultaneously or concurrently available, each with its own schedule of reward, is called a *concurrent schedule of reinforce-*

ment. Behavior on concurrent schedules of reinforcement is very interesting. Let's say, for example, that the researcher has arranged the experiment so that the rat gets a food pellet after every five chain pulls and gets a food pellet after every ten lever presses. We now have a simplified laboratory model that yields information about how the rat distributes his behavior across various alternatives. Will the rat spend all of his time pulling the chain? Or will he spend most of his time pulling the chain? Or will he spend all of his time pressing the lever? In short, what will the animal choose to do?

Research in these more complex Skinner Box arrangements has now been going on for about thirty years. The results of this type of experimentation, whether with rats, pigeons, hamsters, monkeys, humans, or a wide variety of other species, are similar. In many cases, it has been found that the "relative" rate of responding matches the "relative" rate of reward. *Relative* here means the amount of one behavior divided by the total amount of all behaviors, or the amount of reward for one behavior divided by the total amount of all rewards. In other words, if the rat gets 33 percent of all of her rewards for chain pulling and 67 percent for lever pressing, she will lever press twice as much as she will chain pull (33 percent of her total behavior will be chain pulling and 67 percent will be lever pressing). This result is referred to as the *Matching Law:* The relative rate of responding matches the relative rate of reward.

Concurrent schedules and the Matching Law present a new way of thinking about such psychological concepts as freedom and choice. Many psychologists have argued that it is possible to develop a science of psychology by studying relationships between behavior and events in the environment. Concepts such as freedom and choice are difficult to study scientifically because they are commonly defined in ways that make them neither behavior nor environmental events. Freedom frequently is defined as a condition in which there are no environmental effects on behavior. Choice commonly is defined as a mental or psychic process.

Concurrent schedules are situations that we typically describe as involving making choices in a free environment. The rat is free to lever press, chain pull, or do nothing. That is its choice. There might be consequences for what the rat does, but isn't that always the case with living things? The results of research on concurrent schedules are described by the Matching Law, which is stated entirely in terms of behavior and rewards. No appeal to an internal choice process is required.

It makes sense to continue to use the word *choice* in describing behavior on concurrent schedules, but it is now defined as behavior in the context of other behavior. What behavior one chooses to engage in varies as a function of relative reinforcement rate. Likewise, *freedom* can be defined as the availability of alternatives. In RAT RACE, rats are not free to run until the experimenter opens the start box door. They can, however, run or not run, and if they chose to run they are free to run at different speeds. The rat, pigeon, or human in a Skinner Box is free to lever press, or not to lever press, to disk peck or not to disk peck, to button press or not to button press. The experimental subject on a concurrent schedule of reward has greater freedom than one in the simple Skinner Box. In the program RAT 1, the rat can lever press or not lever press.

In program RAT 2, the rat can lever press, chain pull, or do nothing; it has, therefore, a greater amount of freedom. By inventing the Skinner Box, Skinner has facilitated the systematic study of choice (behavior in the context of other behavior) and freedom (the availability of alternatives).

Many Artificial Behavior applications require individuals who are free to make choices. A simulation of a concurrent reward schedule in a Skinner Box can illustrate the programming necessary to instantiate such procedures. First, a formal model of the relationships between behavior and its consequences is necessary to produce such a simulation.

Earlier in this chapter, reference was made to the Matching Law as a rule for describing the results of research involving freely responding individuals in situations where several behaviors are available. The Matching Law is a general description of the relationship between behavior and its consequences that applies only after the individual has had a large amount of experience in the situation. It was not developed from studying moment-by-moment changes in behavior but by looking at large amounts of behavior, and reward, accumulated over large amounts of time. Whether or not it is capable of describing moment-to-moment changes in behavior as a function of single rewards is still an open question.

We do know that behavior does not always fit the Matching Law. We will continue to use the psychological model for the effects of reward on behavior that was developed in Chapters 3, 4, 5, and 6 for our simulation of a concurrent schedule of reward. Research currently is underway to test the applicability of that model to data from complex schedules of rewards. In some cases, the model does predict matching of relative responding and relative rate of reward, but other times it yields deviations from strict matching. Early research results suggest that this model describes a larger amount of data than the Matching Law.

Our model, which says that rewards increase expectations according to the formula $\Delta E = F(O - E)$, that nonreward when reward is expected increases frustration according to the same formula, and that reward when frustration is present produces courage, will be referred to as DMOD throughout the rest of the book. The acronym DMOD represents Daly Model, after its authors Helen and John Daly.

DMOD will be used in program RAT 2 to calculate the effects of reward and nonreward on lever pressing and chain pulling. In addition, some new graphics are required for the chain, and animation of the chain-pulling behavior.

PROGRAM DESCRIPTION

Program RAT 2 begins to push the limits of what we can do on the APPLE without getting into memory management and alternative graphics and animation techniques. For this reason, all REMarks have been removed from RAT 2. RAT 2 uses the same main screen drawing as RAT 1 so lines 3020 through 3420, which draw the rat in the Skinner Box, are the same as RAT 1. Lines 500 through 610 for animating the bar-press response also are the same as in RAT 1. You can create RAT 2 by loading RAT 1 and deleting and adding lines as listed below.

Line 110 calls the subroutine at line 3020 for drawing the rat in the Skinner Box on the screen. This subroutine is the same as RAT 1 with the addition of the chain and ring at line 3310. Since we now have two behaviors, lever pressing and chain pulling, all of the variables in the psychological model, E1 to E3, and T1 to T4, are now subscripted with the variable Z. When a lever press occurs, $Z = 1$ and calculations are carried out for changes in expectation of reward, frustration, and courage for lever pressing. They also are accumulated in variables T1(Z) to T3(Z), and a total response strength is calculated, T4(Z). When a chain pull occurs, $Z = 2$ and the same calculations are carried out for E1(Z) to E3(Z) and for T1(Z) to T4(Z). There are now two vectors of immediate and accumulated effects of reward and nonreward, one vector for each of the two behaviors.

PROGRAM VARIABLES

E1(1)—expectation of reward for lever pressing

E2(1)—expectation of frustration for lever pressing

E3(1)—courage to lever press in the face of expectation of frustration

T1(1)—accumulated expectation of reward for lever pressing

T2(1)—accumulated expectation of frustration for lever pressing

T3(1)—accumulated courage to lever press

T4(1)—expectation, minus frustration, plus courage for lever pressing

E1(2)—expectation of reward for chain pulling

E2(2)—expectation of frustration for chain pulling

E3(2)—courage to chain pull in the face of expectation of frustration
for chain pulling

T1(2)—accumulated expectation of reward for chain pulling

T2(2)—accumulated expectation of frustration for chain pulling

T3(2)—accumulated courage to chain pull

T4(2)—expectation, minus frustration, plus courage for chain pulling

Line 0120 sets T1(1), T4(1), T1(2), and T4(2) equal to 0.05. This means that the rat begins with a very small tendency to press the lever and an exactly equal small tendency to pull the chain. Line 0150 sets other variables equal to 0. The variable S is set equal to (-16336). This is the value that will be used to toggle the Apple's speaker for sound effects.

Line 0160 increments the variable PL by 1. As in program RAT 1, this will be used to subscript the RND function to generate random numbers. This line also clears the register for the keyboard strobe (-16368) to 0. Lines 0170 through 0200 convert T4(1) and T4(2) to integers and multiply them times 0.75, and then assign that value to the variables T5(1) and T5(2). When total response strength reaches 1.00 (T5 = 1.00, for example), as you have seen it do in RAT RACE, RAT 1, and PIGEON 1, the other behavior would not occur in RAT 2. Since the interaction of expectations, frustration, and courage can produce values of T4 greater than 1.00, and in real life that rarely precludes the occurrence of other behaviors, we will use 0.75 times the calculated value of T5 to determine the probability of that behavior. This preserves the possibility of other behaviors occurring unless the simulated individual has acquired a grossly inordinate response strength. When this occurs in real life, we describe the person as compulsive.

Lines 0210 through 0240, 0280 through 0320, and 0350 through 0380 check the keyboard for user input and then evaluate it. As in program RAT 1, if the user has hit the S key, AA = 211 and the program stops, while if the user has pressed the R key, AA = 210, and the next lever press will be followed by a reward. In RAT 2, if the user presses the U key, AA = 213, and the next chain pull response will be followed by a food reward.

Line 0250 generates a random number, and converts it to an integer value. If the random number (RN) is from 0 to 50, the program control branches to line 320. Line 320 evaluates a new random number generated at line 270, and if it is less than T5(1) control branches to line 500, which is the routine for animating a lever press. If the random number generated at line 260 is from 51 to 100, control skips to line 330. A new random number is generated at line 330. At line 340, if the random number is less than T5(2), control branches to line 710, which is the routine for animating a chain pull. If no behavior occurs, lines 390 and 400 return control to line 210, where the entire process begins again. If a lever press or chain pull occurs, Z is set to 1 or 2 as appropriate and the calculation routine beginning at line 920 calculates changes in response strength for the appropriate behavior.

The calculation of the psychological constructs at lines 920 through 1090 is exactly as it is in RAT RACE 3, RAT 1, and PIGEON 1. The subscript Z after each variable is used to keep track of the psychological values for the two behaviors: Z = 1 is lever pressing and Z = 2 is chain pulling. After these calculations are carried out, control is returned to line 0150, where the entire routine starts anew.

PROGRAM LISTING

Load program RAT 1 and delete the following list of line numbers. Do not worry about RAT 1; it is still on your disk. We are simply using much of the graphics in RAT 1 to create RAT 2. You will save the new program under the name RAT 2.

```
            DELETE Lines 100 TO 490

            DELETE Lines 700 TO 3010

            DELETE Lines  540

                              550

                              560

                             3030

                             3050

                             3160

                             3170

                             3210

                             3250
```

Now ADD (by typing in) the following new lines:

```
0110    GOSUB 3020
0120    T1(1) = .05:T4(1) = .05:T1(2) = .05:T4(2) = .05
0150    R(1) = 0:R(2) = 0:RN = 0:AA = 0:S = ( - 16336):PL = 0:
        X = FRE (0)
0160    PL = PL + 1:POKE - 16368,0
0170    T5(1) = INT (100 * T4(1))
0180    T5(1) = INT (.75 * T5(1))
0190    T5(2) = INT (100 * T4(2))
0200    T5(2) = INT (.75 * T5(2))
0210    FOR K = 1 TO 100:AA = PEEK ( - 16384):NEXT K
0220    IF AA = 210 THEN R(1) = 1
0230    IF AA = 213 THEN R(2) = 1
0240    IF AA = 211 THEN GOTO 2900
0250    RN = INT (100 * RND (PL))
0260    IF RN > 50 THEN GOTO 330
0270    PL = PL + 1:RN = INT (100 * RND (PL))
0280    AA = PEEK ( - 16384)
0290    IF AA = 210 THEN R(1) = 1
0300    IF AA = 213 THEN R(2) = 1
0310    IF AA = 211 THEN GOTO 2900
0320    IF RN < T5(1) THEN GOTO 500
0330    PL = PL + 1:RN = INT (100 * RND (PL))
0340    IF RN < T5(2) THEN GOTO 710
0350    AA = PEEK ( - 16384)
0360    IF AA = 210 THEN R(1) = 1
0370    IF AA = 213 THEN R(2) = 1
0380    IF AA = 211 THEN GOTO 2900
0390    IF R(1) = 1 THEN GOTO 210
0400    IF R(2) = 1 THEN GOTO 210
0410    GOTO 160
```

```
0550   FOR BEEP = 1 TO 10:SOUND = PEEK (S):NEXT BEEP


0670   IF R(1) = 1 THEN GOSUB 1220
0680   Z = 1
0690   GOTO 910
0710   HCOLOR = 0:HPLOT 71,132 TO 78,132:HPLOT 75,131 TO 85,131:
       HPLOT 77,130 TO 79,130:HPLOT 85,130 TO 88,130:HPLOT
       77,127 TO 78,127 TO 78,126 TO 81,126:HPLOT 79,125 TO
       82,125:HPLOT 80,124 TO 83,124:HPLOT 81,123
0720   HPLOT 84,124 TO 72,131:HPLOT 85,124 TO 71,132:HPLOT
       86,124 TO 72,132
0730   HPLOT 118,102 TO 131,102:HPLOT 127,103 TO 138,103:
       HPLOT 141,104 TO 134,104 TO 134,105 TO 143,105:HPLOT
       144,106 TO 142,106 TO 142,107 TO 145,107:HCOLOR = 3:
       HPLOT 96,106 TO 89,106:HPLOT 100,105 TO 91,105:HPLOT
       102,104 TO 94,104
0740   HPLOT 99,103 TO 109,103:HPLOT 108,102 TO 110,102:HPLOT
       81,119 TO 78,119 TO 78,120 TO 82,120:HPLOT 80,121 TO
       81,121 TO 81,122:HPLOT 71,109 TO 71,106:HPLOT 70,107 TO
       70,105 TO 69,105 TO 69,107:HPLOT 68,105 TO 68,103
       TO 67,103
0750   HCOLOR = 0:HPLOT 64,96:HPLOT 63,97:HPLOT 66,97:HPLOT
       62,98:HPLOT 67,98:HPLOT 61,99 TO 61,100:HPLOT 68,99 TO
       68,100:HPLOT 62,101 TO 62,102
0760   HPLOT 67,101 TO 67,102:HPLOT 63,103:HPLOT 66,103:HPLOT
64,104 TO 65,104
0770   HCOLOR=3:HPLOT 64,99:HPLOT 63,100:HPLOT 66,100:HPLOT
       62,101:HPLOT 67,101:HPLOT 61,102 TO 61,103:HPLOT 68,102
       TO 68,103:HPLOT 62,104 TO 62,105
0780   HPLOT 67,104 TO 67,105:HPLOT 63,106:HPLOT 66,106:HPLOT
       64,107 TO 65,107:HPLOT 65,97 TO 65,99
0790   FOR BEEP = 1 TO 6:SOUND = PEEK (S):NEXT BEEP:FOR I =
       1 TO 100:NEXT I
0800   HCOLOR = 0:HPLOT 67,104 TO 67,105:HPLOT 63,106:HPLOT
       66,106:HPLOT 64,107 TO 65,107:HPLOT 65,97 TO 65,99
0810   HPLOT 64,99:HPLOT 63,100:HPLOT 66,100:HPLOT 62,101:HPLOT
       67,101:HPLOT 61,102 TO 61,103:HPLOT 68,102 TO 68,103:
       HPLOT 62,104 TO 62,105
0820   HCOLOR = 3:HPLOT 67,101 TO 67,102:HPLOT 63,103:HPLOT
       66,103:HPLOT 64,104 TO 65,104
0830   HPLOT 64,96:HPLOT 63,97:HPLOT 66,97:HPLOT 62,98:HPLOT
       67,98:HPLOT 61,99 TO 61,100:HPLOT 68,99 TO 68,100:
       HPLOT 62,101 TO 62,102
0840   HCOLOR = 0:HPLOT 99,103 TO 109,103:HPLOT 108,102 TO
       110,102:HPLOT 81,119 TO 78,119 TO 78,120 TO 82,120:HPLOT
       80,121 TO 81,121 TO 81,122:HPLOT 71,109 TO 71,106:HPLOT
       70,107 TO 70,105 TO 69,105 TO 69,107:HPLOT 68,105 TO
       68,103 TO 67,103
0850   HPLOT 96,106 TO 89,106:HPLOT 100,105 TO 91,105:HPLOT
       102,104 TO 94,104:HCOLOR = 3:HPLOT 118,102 TO 131,102:
       HPLOT 127,103 TO 138,103:HPLOT 141,104 TO 134,104 TO
       134,105 TO 143,105:HPLOT 144,106 TO 142,106 TO 142,107
       TO 145,107
```

```
0860    HPLOT 85,126 TO 71,131 TO 85,127 TO 71,132 TO 85,128:
        HPLOT 75,130 TO 85,130
0870    HPLOT 71,132 TO 78,132:HPLOT 75,131 TO 85,131:HPLOT
        77,130 TO 79,130:HPLOT 85,130 TO 88,130:HPLOT 77,127 TO
        78,127 TO 78,126 TO 81,126:HPLOT 79,125 TO 82,125:HPLOT
        80,124 TO 83,124:HPLOT 81,123:HCOLOR = 3
0880    IF R(2) = 1 THEN GOSUB 1220
0890    Z = 2
0910    IF Z = 2 THEN GOTO 925
0920    IF R(1) = 0 THEN O = 0
0921    IF R(1) = 1 THEN O = 1
0922    GOTO 930
0925    IF R(2) = 0 THEN O = 0
0926    IF R(2) = 1 THEN O = 1
0930    IF O < T1(Z) THEN GOTO 990
0940    E1(Z) = .05 * (O - T1(Z))
0950    IF T2(Z) < = O THEN GOTO 1050
0960    E2(Z) = .01 * ( O - T2(Z))
0970    E3(Z) = .05 * ( T2(Z) - T3(Z))
0980    GOTO 1050
0990    OX = ABS (2 * ( O - T1(Z)))
1000    E2(Z) = .05 * ( OX - T2(Z))
1010    IF T1(Z) < O THEN GOTO 1050
1020    E1(Z) = .01 * (O - T1(Z))
1030    IF E2(Z) < = O THEN GOTO 1050
1040    E3(Z) = .01 * ( O - T3(Z))
1050    T1(Z) = (T1(Z) + E1(Z))
1060    T2(Z) = (T2(Z) + E2(Z))
1070    T3(Z) = (T3(Z) + E3(Z))
1080    T4(Z) = (T4(Z) + (E1(Z) - (E2(Z) / 2) + E3(Z)))
1090    PRINT:PRINT:PRINT "EXPECTATION LEVER = "T4(1):PRINT
        "EXPECTATION CHAIN = "T4(2)
1110    GOTO 150
1220    S = ( -16336):FOR BEEP = 1 TO 4:SOUND = PEEK (S):
        NEXT BEEP
1230    HCOLOR = 3:HPLOT 61,114
1250    HCOLOR = 3:HPLOT 63,114 TO 67,114:HPLOT 64,115 TO
        65,115:HCOLOR = 0:HPLOT 64,117 TO 66,117:HPLOT 65,118 TO
        67,118:HPLOT 66,119 TO 69,119:HPLOT 61,114
1260    HCOLOR = 0:HPLOT 63,114 TO 67,114:HPLOT 64,115 TO 65,115:
        HCOLOR = 3:HPLOT 64,117 TO 66,117:HPLOT 65,118 TO 67,118:
        HPLOT 66,119 TO 69,119
1290    RETURN
2900    TEXT:HOME:END



3310    HPLOT 65,10 TO 65,96:HPLOT 64,96:HPLOT 63,97:HPLOT 66,97:
        HPLOT 62,98:HPLOT 67,98:HPLOT 61,99 TO 61,100:HPLOT
        68,99 TO 68,100:HPLOT 62,101 TO 62,102:HPLOT 67,101 TO
        67,102:HPLOT 63,103:HPLOT 66,103:HPLOT 64,104 TO 65,104
3500    RETURN
```

INSTRUCTIONS FOR USING THE PROGRAM

After you have entered the program and debugged it, you should save it on a tape or disk. Now you are ready to RUN the program. When the program begins, there will be a very small probability $(0.05 \times 0.75 = 0.0375)$ that either lever pressing or chain pulling will occur every time the program goes through the main control loop (lines 120 through 410). You will have to wait some seconds (sometimes as long as a minute or two) for behavior to occur. If you press the R key during this interval, the next lever press will be followed by food, and if you press the U key the next chain pull will be followed by food.

The value of T4 is displayed at the bottom of the screen following each occurrence of a lever press or chain pull. This is the variable the program uses to calculate when the next chain pull or lever press will occur. It is referred to as total expectation or response strength. The screen display reads

"EXPECTATION LEVER = " (T4(1))
"EXPECTATION CHAIN = " (T4(2)).

EXAMPLES AND APPLICATIONS

Program RAT 2 begins to illustrate the power that selection by consequences has to explain the subtleties of naturally occurring behavior. The rat is free to lever press, chain pull, or do nothing. The program user is free to reward lever pressing or chain pulling. When you first run the program, one behavior will occur before the other. The sequence of occurrence is, however, random (although both behaviors have equal probabilities of occurrence). When the first response occurs, you will reward it or not reward it. If you reward it, the animal will be quite surprised and the value of T4 (total expectation of reward for that behavior) will increase substantially. If you now decide to reward the second behavior, to make the two have equal strength, you will press the key to reward the next occurrence of the second behavior, but the first behavior might recur. If this happens, the first behavior will not be rewarded and frustration will occur. The next time this behavior is rewarded, some frustration will be expected, reward will occur, and courage will be learned. You will find that you will soon be unable to keep track of the response strengths of the two behaviors. If you set yourself a goal of keeping the responses equally likely, you can use the values of T4 at the bottom of the screen and attempt to match them. This can be done readily by titrating your delivery of rewards for the two behaviors until the values of T4(1) and T4(2) are approximately equal and the two behaviors occur at approximately the same rate. However, if you stop delivering the rewards you will see that one behavior typically goes away much more rapidly than the other.

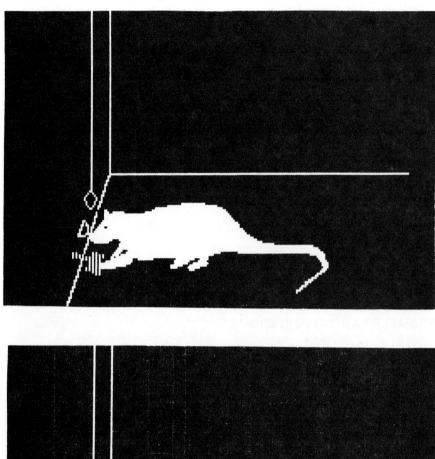

Figure 7-1.   Illustration from program RAT 2. In the top picture, the rat is pressing the lever. In the bottom picture, the rat is pulling on the chain. Both behaviors can be followed by food reward at the discretion of the program user.

This will be the one with the smaller amount of courage learned. One behavior inevitably has a larger value of courage (T3), which decreases at the same rate as expectation of reward (T1). Since expectations and courage decrease more slowly than frustration increases (0.01 versus 0.05), the behavior that reached its value of T4 under more varied conditions of reward and nonreward will be much slower to reduce its frequency even when food reward is withdrawn. The rat will appear to take on a life of its own. It will chain pull, for example, when you have just rewarded lever pressing and when you predict lever-pressing behavior. It might persist in lever pressing when you predict chain pulling. Despite the simplicity of the psychological model, your ability to predict the behavior of the rat is substantially reduced in program RAT 2.

It is in program RAT 2 that you will begin to see the power of Artificial Behavior. If you use this program to learn how the simple psychological model developed in Chapters 3, 4, and 5 can be applied to complex situations, you will be quite surprised. Recall that our model follows a very simple set of rules. When reward occurs, the expectation of reward is incremented as a fraction of the magnitude of the difference between obtained and expected reward $(O - E+)$. If reward does not occur, its expectation is decremented and frustration is incremented as a fraction of the difference between expected reward and frustration $(E+ \ - \ E-)$. If reward does occur and frustration is expected, courage is acquired as a function of the difference between expected frustration and already acquired courage $(E- \ - \ C)$.

Earlier chapters demonstrated how these rules could produce depression and elation in a single behavior as a function of the sequence of rewards, nonrewards, and shifts in reward amount. In program RAT 2, we apply these simple rules to two behaviors in the same freely responding individual, and we quickly lose track of our ability to predict the behavior of the graphics simulation. It is quite tempting when using RAT 2 to describe the rat as doing things because "it wants to" or "because it chooses to." The simulated rat's behavior appears to be spontaneous and realistic.

It is important to note here that the generation of random numbers in the program is not the source of the unpredictability. The first random number the program generates (line 250) is used to check the response strengths of the two behaviors equally often. Half of the values are used to branch to checking the response strength for lever pressing and half for chain pulling. This simply keeps the program checking the values of T4(1) and T4(2) equally often. Since the Apple has only one central processing unit, we simply divide its time in half for evaluating response strength of the two behaviors. The random numbers generated at lines 270 and 330 are used to decide whether to lever press or chain pull at any particular moment. These have the effect of producing a temporal distribution of behavior that covaries exactly with the deterministic value of T4 calculated by our psychological model. The larger the value of T4, the denser that distribution is for any given amount of time. This is just a programming technique for instantiating an animated graphics representation of two behaviors. So while program RAT 2 applies the simple psychological model employing three constructs (expectations, frustration, and courage) to an individual with only two behaviors and one type of reward, the computer simulation demonstrates how the simple model can describe very complex patterns of behavior. With RAT 2, many applications of AB techniques begin to get exciting. I now will discuss educational applications, followed by a discussion of applications in research and computer games.

Educational Applications

In teaching the effects of reward on behavior, it is useful to go through the three versions of program RAT RACE before developing more complex examples. This experience allows the students to observe at firsthand the development of expectations, the operation of frustration, and the learning of courage in a well-controlled environment. These simulations give the students immediate feedback about the effects of reward and nonreward on behavior. They also provide illustrations of how certain sequences of rewards can produce such effects as depression, elation, and resistance to change.

Moving then to either program RAT 1 or PIGEON 1 can demonstrate how difficult it becomes to follow the operation of these effects in a free responding situation. Students quickly realize how simple laws relating behavior and its consequences might govern freely responding individuals. They will, however, typically raise the issues discussed at the beginning of this chapter: "What about the fact that humans can choose what to do?" and "What about the fact that humans are free to choose from a wide variety of alternatives?" Program RAT 2 begins to provide answers to those questions. The rat can now chain pull or lever press to earn a food reward. Pressing the R key rewards lever pressing and pressing the U key rewards chain pulling. I let the students simply play with the program for a while. Then I ask them how well they can predict the rat's behavior: "How many of you found yourself describing the rat as doing what he wanted to, or being free to choose to do whatever he felt like doing?"

The study of the relationship between behavior and its consequences has always been criticized for its apparent simplicity. However, in RAT 2 we find that those relationships can quite quickly produce patterns of behavior that are difficult to predict. We find ourselves using the "wants" or "feelings" of the rat to explain his behavior. The simulated rat, however, contains no "wants" or "feelings" in the sense in which we typically use those terms. This generation of hypothesized explanations for the simulated rat's behavior is instructive. It is relatively commonplace for us to generate concepts to explain behavior. We attribute to individuals states of achievement, motivation, extroversion, intelligence, ego strength, and a long list of unobservable states to try to explain their behavior. If our terms are successful at predicting behavior only some of the time, we are partially rewarded for using them. As you now know, partial reward produces behavior that is very resistant to change. Perhaps we will be able to improve our ability to predict behavior by analyzing how experience with rewards gives rise to patterns of behavior we refer to with terms such as *intelligence* and *introversion*.

In educational settings, it is useful for two people to work together with the program. One person can control the program by pressing the keys to reward the two responses, and the other can write down the sequence of events. The second person might, for example, start with a piece of paper ruled into four columns. The four columns could be used to tally lever presses, chain pulls, rewards for lever pressing, and rewards for chain pulling. They might do this for about twenty or thirty minutes. If they analyze these observations, they will find that in most cases the behavior conforms to the Matching Law. Chain pulling, divided by chain pulling plus lever pressing, will reduce to a fraction approximately equal to rewards for chain pulling divided by the total number of rewards. In general, the relative rate of responding matches the relative rate of reward. However, there will be some exceptions. These exceptions to matching can be examined by having the person writing down the events record each event in sequence, and then running the sequence of rewards for lever pressing and the sequence for chain pulling through the two rats running in program RAT RACE 3. In RAT RACE 3, the free responding situation is brought under control by the program user because he or she controls the availability of the running response and can write down values of expectations after each occurrence of the behavior.

What one learns from these exercises is invaluable in understanding behavior. First, it is difficult for one person both to make observations of rewards and behavior in a complex setting and to conduct a successful behavior change program based on those observations. Such a program will require recording of observations of behavior and rewards, analysis of those data, and then management of the delivery of rewards. Each of these three steps must be ongoing to implement effective teaching, therapy, or any kind of behavior management.

Research Applications

Program RAT 2 suggests some interesting ideas about ways to test the correspondence between a theoretical model and the actual behavior of living subjects. Thus far, the experimental analysis of behavior has concentrated on two types of theory and two types of data. The rat runway procedure has been used to test predictions from theories that are frequently verbal and to make predictions about relatively small amounts of experience. Such theories and procedures have been used to study human behavior as well. Skinner Box procedures have been used to test predictions from quantitative theories about relationships between large amounts of behavior and their consequences, accumulated over large periods of time.

Programs RAT 1, PIGEON 1, and RAT 2 are examples of the extension of a theory developed to describe moment-by-moment changes in behavior to procedures used to study the relationship between large amounts of behavior and large amounts of reward. Program RAT 2 could be easily modified to print out the protocol of responses, rewards, and calculated quantities in the model. This output could be compared to a similar output protocol from a computer-controlled Skinner Box containing a real rat and real food. Ideally, RAT 1, RAT 2, or PIGEON 1 could be rewritten as a real-time simulation. Then the computer controlling the delivery of rewards to the real animal also could signal rewards to the real-time simulation. The stored protocols for the real and simulated animals could be converted to graphic form and compared as a kind of goodness-of-fit test. Similar procedures could be developed to study human behavior, either in the laboratory or in the real world.

Computer Games Applications

Program RAT 2 gives you a believable example of some of the implications of AB techniques for computer games first discussed at the end of Chapter 5. RAT 2 contains a two-unit vector (Z) of behaviors. Each of the values (1 and 2) of the vector calls an animation subroutine for its appropriate response (lever pressing and chain pulling). The user controls the consequences of the behaviors (food or no food), and the program calculates a new value of response strength for each behavior after it occurs. This quantity is used to determine the frequency with which each behavior will occur in the future. If the animated character were a knight, if the behaviors were dragon slaying and note reading, and if the reinforcers were dead dragons and game clues, we would begin to have the outline of an interactive adventure game in which the behavior of the character was based on our knowledge of the relationship between behavior and its consequences. If slaying dragons did not help save the kidnapped princess, a player would learn that from repeated playing of the game. Or if a player were not inclined to save the princess, he might just play the game for the opportunity to slay dragons. In principle, there is no reason for the vector Z to be limited to two behaviors. An interactive computer game might have, for example, six display scenes, six behaviors, and six sources of reward available for each of three characters in each scene. The possibilities are intriguing.

RAT 2 contains only two behaviors for very pragmatic reasons. Throughout the present book, every effort has been made to make Artificial Behavior programming ideas and techniques available to the widest possible audience of readers. These programs can be entered from the keyboard in BASIC, and SAVEd, LOADed, and RUN with minimal knowledge of animation and memory management techniques on the Apple. If the programs were much longer, parts or all of the routines would have to be stored above the high-resolution graphics display area of your Apple's memory to prevent the programs from interfering with the graphics displays. However, with some additional skills at memory management and graphics animation, the type of interactive animated adventure game described in the previous paragraph can be implemented on most microcomputers.

SUMMARY

Criticisms of laboratory procedures for the study of behavior center on their simplicity. These procedures can, however, be increased in complexity by adding additional environmental objects to manipulate and additional sources of reward. Program RAT 2 simulates a rat in a Skinner Box who is free to pull a chain or press a lever for food reward. The program user controls food rewards for both behaviors. This program simulates choice, or behavior in the context of other behavioral alternatives. It also simulates freedom by increasing the number of behaviors that are available to the simulated animal. Program RAT 2 illustrates how a few simple rules describing the effects of reward on behavior, in a situation in which two behaviors can occur, produces a simulation that appears to take on a life of its own. RAT 2, and suitable extensions of its logic, can be used to instruct people about the complexities produced by the relationship between behavior and its consequences, to develop simulations to compare the fit of formal models to the behavior of real individuals, and to develop interactive, animated computer adventure games with lifelike appearances.

ADDITIONAL READINGS

The following book chapter presents very interesting conceptual and laboratory research on the concept of freedom.

1. Catania, A. C. "Freedom of Choice: A Behavioral Analysis," in G. H. Bower (ed.) *The Psychology of Learning and Motivation,* Vol. 14 (New York: Academic Press, 1980).

These papers review and summarize a large amount of research which can be described by the Matching Law.

2. deVilliers, P. A., and Herrnstein, R. J., "Toward a Law of Response Strength," *Psychological Bulletin,* 1976, *83,* pp. 1131–53.
3. deVilliers, P. A., "Choice in Concurrent Schedules and a Quantitative Formulation of the Law of Effect," in W. K. Honig and J. E. R. Staddon (eds.), *Handbook of Operant Behavior* (Englewood Cliffs, N.J.: Prentice-Hall, Inc., 1977).
4. Nye, R. D., *What is B. F. Skinner Really Saying?* (Englewood Cliffs, N.J.: Prentice-Hall, Inc., 1979).
5. Skinner, B. F., *Walden Two* (New York: MacMillan, 1948).

8

DISCRIMINATION, CORRELATION, SUPERSTITION
Program
Rat's Alley

In the November 1983 issue of *Antic,* a magazine for Atari computer users, Electronic Arts ran a full-page advertisement with a large typeface header reading "Bill Budge wants to write a computer program so human that turning it off would be an act of murder." The advertisement contained text intended to convince the reader that Mr. Budge (a premier Apple programmer) is capable of developing such a program. In the text of the advertisement, Budge is quoted as saying, "Creating the illusion of personality means creating an intelligence that's always changing. It reacts differently to different situations."

What Budge is saying has considerable surface validity. People read in libraries and bowl in bowling alleys. They listen at concerts and sing in church. Someone who only listens in church, sings while in a concert audience, reads at the bowling alley, and bowls in the library is usually labeled as having minimal discriminable capabilities, as being a deranged personality, or lacking in intellectual capacity. Few of us behave the same way in the presence of our grandmother as we do when we are with our friends. We strike tennis balls with a hand-held racket and soccer balls with our feet, shoulders, or head. Laboratory rats run in runways and press levers in Skinner Boxes. No doubt, if a laboratory rat ran in a Skinner Box or tried to press levers in a runway, someone would label the rat as lacking in intellect or having a deranged personality. In this chapter, we will review some ideas from psychology about this situational specificity of behavior and then develop a technique for including them in Artificial Behavior programs.

The observation that behavior is situationally specific is a common one. For many centuries, philosophers and psychologists have explained the phenomenon by positing that there are connections or associations in people between neural representations of sensations and behavior. Some of these nervous system associations may be genetically prewired and some may be acquired by experience. In either case, the belief is that the nervous system is a repository of an elaborate network of associations that ensure that only certain behaviors occur in certain situations. Stimulation from the environment enters the nervous system from sense organs—eyes, ears, skin, and so on. The sensory nerves are then somehow connected to other nerves that govern behavioral output. The strength of the connections or associations vary from very weak to very strong. The strength of the association between sensory inputs from a library and bowling behavior is, for example, very weak (unless, of course, one is reading books about bowling). The strength of the association between sitting in the audience at a concert and listening is strong. This way of thinking about the situational specificity of behavior has dominated psychology so much that large parts of the cerebral cortex, anatomically dominant in humans, are called association areas. Situational specificity of behavior, the hypothesis of nervous system associations, and intelligent behavior, are all closely related areas of research and investigation. The concept of associations is a part of the formal model of psychological processes presented in earlier chapters of this book.

In both RAT RACE and the free responding RAT 1, the effect of food on the animal increased his expectation of food. But is this expectation of food identical in both cases, and if it is, why does one rat run and the other rat press a lever? DMOD assumes, as have almost all theories of reward and punishment, that reward strengthens an association between the runway and running behavior in one case, and an association between the Skinner Box and lever pressing in the other. DMOD is a theory about the changes in associations between situational events and behavior as a function of reward outcomes. It has been possible to develop the previous AB programs without raising this issue because in all of those programs the situation is constant. To develop Artificial Behavior programs that "create the illusion of personality" by "reacting differently to different situations," it is necessary to incorporate the existing knowledge of associations between situations and behavior into our computer programs.

Again, basic researchers in psychology study the situational specificity of behavior by creating extremely simple models in the laboratory. Since expectations are assumed to be situation specific, researchers have simply manipulated various aspects of the situation during the study of reinforcement and observed the behavior changes of their research subjects. In order to manipulate aspects of a situation, they usually add such simple events as lights or sounds. At small intensities, these stimuli are thought to be affectively neutral. They are not in themselves rewards or punishments, but they can be manipulated in such a way that they become predictors of rewards and nonrewards. Such procedures constitute the study of discrimination learning.

Suppose, for example, we turn on a light in the goal box of a runway every time reward is present and do not turn the light on if the reward is absent. With experience, the rat will come to run rapidly when the light is on and slowly when the light is off. In a real-life situation, we humans also may react to situational changes. We may do a good job when the boss is smiling but only an adequate job when the boss is frowning. Since the behavior in both cases covaries with the stimulus (light or facial expression), we say that the behavior is under stimulus control of the light or facial expression. (*Stimulus control* is the research psychologists' technical term that refers to situational specificity of behavior.)

In the rat example, we describe the behavior as indicative of a state of knowledge. The rat knows that when the light is on she will be rewarded and when the light is off she will not be rewarded. As workers, we know that when the boss is smiling he will be openly pleased with our work, but when the boss is frowning he won't like what we have done, no matter how good our work is. Stimulus control helps us understand such things as the formation of discriminations and states of knowledge, such as superstition, correlation, and the comprehension of causal relationships (to name only a few cognitive or stimulus control activities). The simulation of stimulus control will help us develop animated graphics characters whose behavior is indicative of an elaborate sensitivity to the environment.

Incorporating stimulus control into a computer simulation is straightforward. As stated in previous presentations of program RAT RACE, there are three major psychological constructs in the simulation model—expectation $(E+)$, frustration $(E-)$, and courage (C). When we change from a constant situation to a variable situation, we simply subscript the three constructs with symbols representing environmental events or stimuli. This subscript was unnecessary as long as there was only one set of situational events present. Consider the subscript value 1 as indicating the runway as a stimulus and the value 2 as the light stimulus. Now we have a vector of situations; in the present case, it has two values, $E+(1)$ now represents the value of expectation of reward associated with the runway, $E+(2)$ the expectation of reward associated with light, and $E+(1) + E+(2)$ the expectation of reward associated with the lighted runway. Psychologists have conducted thousands of studies to find out how these situationally specific expectations are acquired.

Results of research on stimulus control will be incorporated into a new program, RAT'S ALLEY. It has been found that the changes in the strength of an association between a particular stimulus and a particular behavior depend on the existing strength of associations of all stimuli present when the behavior occurs. This can be stated symbolically for our runway/light case as

$$\Delta E+(1) = F(O-(E+(1) + E+(2))$$

This formula says that the increment in the expectation of reward for running in the runway is equal to a fraction of the difference between the obtained reward and existing expectations associated with the runway plus existing expectation associated with the light. And

$$\Delta E+(2) = F(O-(E+(2) + E+(1))$$

This means that if the runway environment is present $(E+(1))$ and the light is on, we must take any association between light and running into account when calculating changes in the association between the runway and running behavior. When determining running speed or animation rate, we must sum the associative strength of all stimuli present at the time.

Programs RAT 1, RAT 2, and RAT 3 displayed two rats in two runways to illustrate the operation of our psychological model. By comparing the behavior of two animals, we may observe the effect on running speed of the presence or absence of various frustration- or courage-inducing experiences. When we study stimulus control, however, we readily can see the effects of situational specificity if we map response strength directly onto the behavior of a single individual and let the program user define the situation as well as the presence or absence of reward. RAT'S ALLEY contains a single runway, one rat, two light sources, and the user can specify the presence or absence of the light stimuli, as well as reward conditions.

DESCRIPTION OF PROGRAM RAT'S ALLEY

Control Program

Lines 100–990

Subroutines

Lines 1000–1050 Draws runways and lampshades
Lines 1200–1230 Draws runway doors
Lines 1300–1340 Draws rat in startbox
Lines 1400–1440 Draws rat in runway
Lines 1600–1680 Dispenses pellets
Lines 1700–1720 Lights red lamp
Lines 1750–1790 Lights green lamp
Lines 2000–2400 Calculations
Lines 2500–2680 Animation
Lines 3000–3130 Input routine

Program RAT'S ALLEY begins by clearing the high-resolution graphics screen and setting the plotting color to white at lines 100 and 110. Line 120 calls the routine at line 1000, which draws the runway and lampshades on the screen. Line 130 calls the subroutine, which draws the doors in the runway, and line 140 calls the subroutine at line 1300, which draws the rat in the start box. Line 150 calls the input routine at line 3000.

The input routine begins by asking the program user if he or she wants the red and/or green lights turned on. If the user answers yes to either, the lights are turned on by calling the appropriate subroutines (line 1700 or line 1750). If the red light is turned on, the variable SR is set equal to 1, and if the green light is turned on, the variable SG is set equal to 1. The input routine then asks how many food pellets to place in the food cup. The variable R is set equal to the number of food pellets. The pellet dispensing routine at line 1600 is identical to the one in program RAT RACE. The last line in the input routine (line 3120) sets the variable NS to equal the number of stimuli present. The runway is always present and a 1 is added if the red and/or green light is on. Therefore, NS can take values from 1 to 3. Program control is then returned to line 160.

Line 160 calls the subroutine to dispense the food pellets on the screen. Line 170 calls the calculation subroutine at line 2000. Lines 2010 and 2015 set the total values of expectation, frustration, and courage (and the temporary values from the previous trial) equal to 0. Lines 2020 through 2050 add the values for expectation, frustration, and courage into the variables represented in the right-hand column of Figure 8-1. If SR = 1 (the red light is on), lines 2070 through

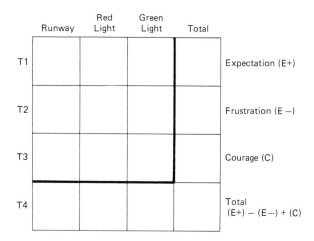

Figure 8-1. Matrix of psychological states (behaviors) and situations (stimuli) used in program RAT'S ALLEY.

2100 add the values from column 2 of Figure 8-1 into column 4. If the red light is off, line 2060 skips control to line 2110. If the green light is on (SG = 1), lines 2120 through 2150 add the values in column 3 of Figure 8-1 to the values in column 4. If the green light is off, control is transferred by line 2110 to line 2160. At this point, the values in the right-hand column of Figure 8-1 are the total values of expectation, frustration, and courage for only the stimuli present on the upcoming running response. Lines 2160 through 2300 now calculate changes in the psychological variables that will occur when the present trial is completed. The calculational routine is the same one used in prior programs. In our general formula $\Delta E = F(O - E)$, the value of expectations that we use on each trial is the accumulated value associated with the stimuli present on that trial. This is why the program recalculates values for the right-hand column of Figure 8-1 for each trial. Those are the values used for current expectations for all trials. Program control now returns to line 180.

Line 180 tells the program user to press any key to begin the animation routine. Following any key press, the computer prints the value of T4(4), the total expectation effecting running rate under the user-defined stimulus conditions, and program control branches to line 1200, which erases the runway doors. Line 230 branches to the animation algorithm at line 2500.

The animation algorithm in RAT'S ALLEY is a different one than was used in RAT RACE. In program RAT RACE, there are two rats on the screen and the crucial point to illustrate is the speed of one rat relative to the other. These comparisons ensure the illustration of the operation of expectations, frustration, and courage. In program RAT'S ALLEY, with only one rat on the screen (and the current expectation printed at the bottom of the screen), the actual running speed varies as response rate did in program RAT 1, PIGEON 1, and RAT 2. Line 2520 converts T4(4) to an integer (T5). Line 2530 begins a

32-count loop. Line 2550 generates a random number and converts it to an integer. At line 2560, if the integer is larger than T5, control is sent back to 2540 to generate another random number. Whenever the random number is less than T5, line 2570 sends control to the actual animation lines beginning at 2650. The animation procedure is the exact one from RAT RACE. After moving the rat five pixels, Y is incremented by 5 and program control is returned to line 2530, where the loop begins again. After the loop has run 32 times, the rat is in front of the food cup and eats the pellets at line 2600. Lines 2602 and 2604 turn off the lights and line 2610 returns control to line 240.

Line 240 branches control to a part of the calculation subroutine at line 2310. Line 2320 divides any changes in expectations, frustration, and courage that occurred on that trial by NS, the number of stimuli present. These values are then added to the appropriate three, six, or nine cells in Figure 8-1 at lines 2330 through 2400. Program control then returns to line 250. Beginning at line 250, this entire sequence begins again as it does in program RAT RACE.

PROGRAM LISTING

```
0100    POKE 230,32:CALL 62450:HGR
0110    HCOLOR = 3
0120    GOSUB 1000
0130    GOSUB 1200
0140    GOSUB 1300
0150    GOSUB 3000
0160    GOSUB 1600
0170    GOSUB 2000
0180    PRINT "PRESS ANY KEY TO START ":GET SS$
0190    PRINT:PRINT "EXPECTATION IS "T4(4)
0200    HCOLOR = 0:GOSUB 1200
0210    GOSUB 1300
0220    Y = 63:HCOLOR = 3:GOSUB 1400
0230    GOSUB 2500
0240    GOSUB 2310
0250    PRINT:PRINT "DO YOU WANT ANOTHER TRIAL? (Y/N)"
0260    INPUT SS$
0270    IF SS$ = "N" THEN GOTO 600
0280    X = 223:Y = 223:HCOLOR = 0
0290    GOSUB 1400
0300    HCOLOR = 3:GOTO 130
0600    TEXT:HOME:END
0990    STOP
1000    REM   DRAWS RUNWAY
1020    HPLOT 220,100 TO 247,100 TO 247,141 TO 220,141 TO 220,
        134 TO 69,134 TO 69,141 TO 43,141 TO 43,100 TO 69,100
        TO 69,107 TO 220,107 TO 220,100
1030    HPLOT 221,101 TO 246,101 TO 246,100 TO 221,140 TO 221,
        133 TO 68,133 TO 68,140 TO 44,140 TO 44,101 TO 68,101
        TO 68,108 TO 221,108 TO 221,101
1040    HPLOT 245,117 TO 240,117 TO 240,125 TO 245,125
```

```
1050    REM   DRAWS LAMPSHADES
1060    HPLOT 110,0 TO 110,79 TO 109,79 TO 109,0:HPLOT 100,80
        TO 119,80:HPLOT 98,81 TO 121,81:HPLOT 97,82 TO 122,82:
        HPLOT 95,83 TO 100,83:HPLOT 119,83 TO 124,83:HPLOT
        90,84 TO 97,84:HPLOT 122,84 TO 129,84
1070    HPLOT 180,0 TO 180,79 TO 179,79 TO 179,0:HPLOT 170,80
        TO 189,80:HPLOT 168,81 TO 191,81:HPLOT 167,82 TO 192,82:
        HPLOT 165,83 TO 170,83:HPLOT 189,83 TO 194,83:HPLOT
        160,84 TO 167,84:HPLOT 192,84 TO 199,84
1080    RETURN
1200    REM   DRAWS DOORS
1220    HPLOT 68,111 TO 68,130 TO 69,130 TO 69,111:HPLOT 220,
        111 TO 220,130 TO
        221,111 TO 221,130
1230    RETURN
1300    REM   DRAWS RAT IN SB
1310    HPLOT 53,117 TO 55,117:HPLOT 51,118 TO 59,118:
        HPLOT 63,118 TO 64,118:HPLOT 50,119 TO 60,119:
        HPLOT 62,119 TO 65,119:HPLOT 49,120 TO 66,120:
        HPLOT 48,121 TO 60,121:HPLOT 62,121 TO 65,121
1320    HPLOT 48,122 TO 49,122:HPLOT 51,122 TO 59,122:HPLOT
        63,122 TO 64,122:HPLOT 48,123:HPLOT 53,123 TO 55,123:
        HPLOT 58,123:HPLOT 48,124:HPLOT 48,125 TO 49,125:HPLOT
        55,125 TO 59,125:HPLOT 49,126 TO 51,126
1330    HPLOT 54,126 TO 55,126:HPLOT 51,127 TO 54,127
1340    RETURN
1400    REM   DRAWS RAT
1410    REM   IN ALLEYWAY
1420    HPLOT Y + 3,117 TO Y + 5,117:HPLOT Y + 8,117::HPLOT
        Y + 1,118 TO Y + 9,118:HPLOT Y + 13,118 TO Y + 14,118:
        HPLOT Y,119 TO Y + 10,119:HPLOT Y + 12,119 TO Y + 15,119:
        HPLOT Y - 1,120 TO Y + 16,120:HPLOT Y - 11,121 TO
        Y + 10,121
1430    HPLOT Y + 12,121 TO Y + 15,121:HPLOT Y - 1, 122 TO
        Y + 9,122:HPLOT Y + 13,122:HPLOT Y + 3,123 TO Y + 5,123:
        HPLOT Y + 8,123
1440    RETURN
1600    REM   DISPENSES PELLETS
1605    IF R = 0 THEN GOTO 1680
1610    Z1 = 120:Z2 = 121
1620    FOR A = 1 TO R
1630    FOR G = 1 TO 5:X= PEEK (-16330):NEXT G
1640    HCOLOR = 3:HPLOT 243,Z1 TO 243,Z2 TO 244,Z2 TO 244,Z1
1645    FOR H = 1 TO 25:NEXT H
1650    HCOLOR = 0:HPLOT 243,Z1 TO 243,Z2 TO 244,Z2 TO 244,Z1
1660    NEXT A
1670    HCOLOR = 3:HPLOT 243,Z1 TO 243,Z2 TO 244,Z2 TO 244,Z1
1680    RETURN
1700    REM   RED LIGHT
1710    HPLOT 103,83 TO 116,83 TO 116,84 TO 103,84:HPLOT
        104,85 TO 115,85:HPLOT 106,86 TO 113,86:HPLOT 106,88
        TO 106,95:HPLOT 112,88 TO 112,95:HPLOT 102,87 TO 95,91:
        HPLOT 117,87 TO 124,91
1720    RETURN
```

```
1750    REM   GREEN LIGHT
1760    HPLOT 173,83 TO 186,83 TO 186,84 TO 173,84:HPLOT  174,85
        TO 185,85:HPLOT 176,86 TO 183,86:HPLOT  177,88 TO 177,
        95:HPLOT 183,88 TO 183,95:HPLOT 172,87 TO 165,91:HPLOT
        187,87 TO 194,91
1790    RETURN
2000    REM   CALCULATION ROUTINE
2010    T1(4) = 0:T2(4) = 0:T3(4) = 0:T4(4)=0
2015    E1 = 0:E2 = 0:E3 = 0
2020    T1(4) = T1(1)
2030    T2(4) = T2(1)
2040    T3(4) = T3(1)
2050    T4(4) = (T1(1) - T2(1) + T3(1))
2060    IF SR = 0 THEN GOTO 2110
2070    T1(4) = T1(4) + T1(2)
2080    T2(4) = T2(4) + T2(2)
2090    T3(4) = T3(4) + T3(2)
2100    T4(4) = T4(4) + (T1(2) - T2(2) +T3(2))
2110    IF SG = 0 THEN GOTO 2160
2120    T1(4) = T1(4) + T1(3)
2130    T2(4) = T2(4) + T2(3)
2140    T3(4) = T3(4) + T3(3)
2150    T4(4) = T4(4) + (T1(3) - T2(3) + T3(3))
2160    O = R * .05:IF O < T1(4)   THEN GOTO 2230
2170    E1 = .15 * (O - T1(4))
2180    IF T2(4) < = 0 THEN GOTO 2300
2190    E2 = .05 * (O - T2(4))
2200    IF T2(4) < = 0 THEN GOTO 2300
2210    E3 = .15 * (T2(4) - T3(4))
2220    GOTO 2300
2230    OX = ABS (2 * (O - T1(4)))
2240    E2 = .15 * (OX - T2(4))
2250    IF T1(4) < 0 THEN GOTO 2300
2260    E1 = .05 * (O - T1(4))
2270    IF E2 < 0 THEN GOTO 2300
2280    E3 = .05 * (O - T3(4))
2300    RETURN
2310    REM ACCUMULATES E'S
2320    E1 = E1/NS:E2 = E2/NS:E3 = E3/NS
2330    T1(1) = T1(1) + E1:T2(1) = T2(1) + E2:T3(1) = T3(1) + E3
2340    IF SR = 0 THEN GOTO 2360
2350    T1(2) = T1(2)+E1:T2(2) = T2(2)+E2:T3(2) = T3(2)+E3
2360    IF SG = 0 THEN GOTO 2400
2370    T1(3) = T1(3)+E1:T2(3) = T2(3)+E2:T3(3) = T3(3) + E3
2400    RETURN
2500    REM   ANIMATION
2510    Y = 63:PL = 0
2520    T5 = INT (100 * T4(4))
2525    IF T5 < 0 THEN T5=0
2530    FOR C = 1 TO 32
2540    PL = PL + 1
2550    T6 = INT (100 * RND(PL))
2560    IF T6 > T5 THEN GOTO 2540
2570    GOSUB 2650
2580    Y = Y + 5
```

```
2590  NEXT C
2600  HCOLOR = 0:HPLOT 243,120 TO 243,121 TO 244,121 TO
      244,120
2602  GOSUB 1700
2604  GOSUB 1750
2610  RETURN
2650  HCOLOR = 0:HPLOT Y + 3,117 TO Y + 5,117:HPLOT Y + 1,118
      TO Y + 5,118:HPLOT Y,119 TO Y + 4,119:HPLOT Y - 1,120
      TO Y + 3,120:HPLOT Y - 11,121 TO Y - 7,121:HPLOT Y - 1,
      122 TO Y + 3,122:HPLOT Y + 3,123 TO Y + 5,123
2660  HCOLOR = 3:HPLOT Y + 9,117 TO Y + 10,117:HPLOT Y + 13,117
      :HPLOT Y + 10,118 TO Y + 12,118:HPLOT Y + 18,118 TO
      Y + 19,118:HPLOT Y + 11,119:HPLOT Y + 17,119 TO Y + 20,
      119:HPLOT Y + 17,120 TO Y + 21,120:HPLOT Y + 11,121
2670  HPLOT Y + 17,121 TO Y + 20,121:HPLOT Y + 10,122 TO Y +
      12,122:HPLOT Y + 18,122 TO Y + 19,122:HPLOT Y + 9,123
      TO Y + 10,123:HPLOT Y + 13,123
2680  RETURN
3000  REM  INPUT ROUTINE
3010  NS = 0:SR = 0:SG = 0
3020  VTAB 24:PRINT:PRINT:PRINT
3030  PRINT "RED LIGHT ON ? (Y/N)":INPUT I$
3040  IF I$ = "Y" THEN HCOLOR = 2
3045  IF I$ = "Y" THEN GOSUB 1700
3050  IF I$ = "Y" THEN SR = 1
3060  PRINT "GREEN LIGHT ON ? (Y/N)":INPUT I$
3070  IF I$ = "Y" THEN HCOLOR = 1
3075  IF I$ = "Y" THEN GOSUB 1750
3076  HCOLOR = 3
3080  IF I$ = "Y" THEN SG = 1
3100  PRINT:PRINT:PRINT "HOW MANY FOOD PELLETS ? (0 TO 20)":
      INPUT R
3110  IF R > 20 THEN GOTO 3100
3120  NS = 1 + SR + SG
3130  RETURN
```

EXAMPLES AND ILLUSTRATIONS

When you RUN program RAT'S ALLEY, it will begin by asking whether you want the red or green light turned on. If you are using a black-and-white monitor, the red light is on the left and the green light is on the right. (You may wish to change the words RED and GREEN to LEFT and RIGHT in lines 3030 and 3060 of the program.) The program will then ask you how many food pellets you want to give the rat on that trial. Before the animation begins, the expectation, based on the associations of all stimuli present, is displayed at the bottom of the screen. The value of expectations on the first trial is 0, no matter what stimuli are present. The value displayed on subsequent trials will always be greater than 0 because the runway stimulus is always present and has been paired with reward.

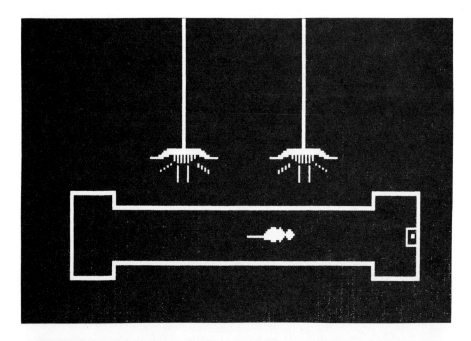

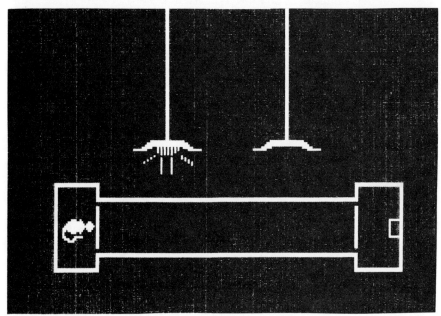

Figure 8-2.   Illustrations from program RAT'S ALLEY. In the top picture, both lights are on, the food is in the food cup, and the rat is scampering down the runway. In the bottom picture, the left light is on, the rat is still in the start box, and the runway doors are closed.

Discrimination Learning

To observe how a discrimination is learned, try the following procedure. On the first trial, have the red light on and deliver twenty food pellets. On the second trial, have the red light off, the green light on, and deliver 0 food pellets. On the third trial, have the red light on and deliver twenty pellets, and on the fourth trial, have the green light on and deliver 0 pellets. Continue alternating trials in this fashion. What you will observe is that on early trials with the green light, which has never been followed by reward, running speed will increase. This is illustrated in Figure 8-3. This happens because the runway stimulus is present on all trials. When the red light is first paired with reinforcement, the increase in expectation of food is associated with the red light and the runway. It takes quite a large amount of experience for the expectation of food to come under the control of only the red light.

With large amounts of discrimination training, the stimulus associated with nonreward will have a negative expectation. This occurs because when the runway and green light are present, the runway has a positive expectancy because it has been paired with the red light and food; therefore, frustration continues to accumulate. This frustration is counteracted by expectation of reward on red-light trials, but it is never counteracted by reward experiences for the green light. This becomes more apparent after a close examination of Figure 8-3.

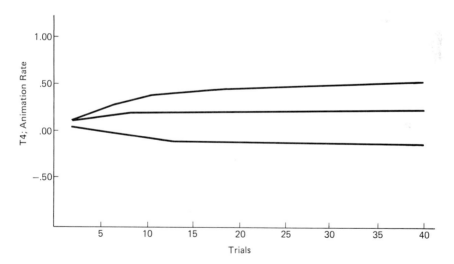

Figure 8-3. Animation rate (response strengths) under the three environmental conditions present during discrimination learning. The top is response strength in the presence of the stimulus paired with reward. The bottom line is response strength controlled by the stimulus never paired with reward, and the middle line is the response strength for the common or background stimulus. The background stimuli are equally paired with reward and no reward, yet always control a level of behavior above zero. This fact is responsible for much superstitious behavior.

These discrimination learning effects may account for a number of day-to-day observations about learning. Consider, for example, a child who is first being taught how to spell. At school, her teacher may give her verbal praise for spelling words correctly. When the child comes home, the environment changes to one in which reward has never been encountered for spelling, but the child walks around the house spelling words. This effect may be mediated by the common stimulus, the presence of adults. The runway is the common stimulus in discrimination learning with the rat in RAT'S ALLEY. It is the runway stimulus that is responsible for the increase in running speed in the presence of the green light even though running has never been rewarded in the presence of the green light. For the child, spelling behavior may increase at home because of the effects of reward on the common stimulus of adults. Many more subtle examples of such effects of discrimination learning can be found around us every day.

It is possible to produce extraordinary running speed in rats by separately reinforcing them in the presence of the red light, and then in the presence of the green light, and finally by presenting both stimuli at once. Try it with the program RAT'S ALLEY, and then ask yourself the question, "What are some examples of this effect in the world outside of the laboratory?"

Depression and Elation

Depression and elation effects presented in Chapters 4 and 5 can be demonstrated with program RAT'S ALLEY. These effects can be much larger and longer lasting if there is a stimulus change that occurs simultaneously with the change in reward conditions. Recall from Chapter 5 that elation occurs when an individual experiences a succession of shifts from large reward to small reward, back to large reward. Try this with RAT'S ALLEY and add a new stimulus at the time of the second shift in reward conditions (the shift that goes from small reward to large reward). This procedure will produce a larger and longer-lasting elation effect than the same procedure without a stimulus change coincident with change in the amount of reward. This simulation is analogous to the effect of first getting a pay reduction at your job, and then taking a new job, in a new setting, at a rate of pay similar to what you were making before the reduction. The new setting will serve to enhance the elation effect produced by the pay raise.

Depression effects that are produced by reward reductions are longer lasting if they are accompanied by a new stimulus. This effect can also be simulated with RAT'S ALLEY.

Blocking

Give the rat in RAT'S ALLEY about fifteen trials with only the red light on and twenty food pellets per trial. What has happened at this point is that the red light and runway have both played a role in the acquisition of the expectation of reward. Now give about five trials with the red light off, the green light on, and twenty food pellets per trial. Notice that expectation is only about half of what it was at the end of the first trials (the ones with the red light). Since so much of the total possible expectation already is associated with the runway, the green light will only generate a small amount of expectation. If we could isolate the green light, away from the runway, it wouldn't control much running behavior at all. This is in spite of the fact that the green light has been present when running was rewarded. Prior stimulus control of running by the red light, and the runway, "blocked" the development of stimulus control by the green light. This is a case where prior learning impedes current learning. If the rat already knows it can obtain food when the red light is on, why bother to learn that the green light also signals food. After all, the rat can already predict the occurrence of the food on the basis of the red light.

Correlation

Some research has suggested that organisms are sensitive to the correlation between stimuli and rewards. Individuals behave as if they are able to detect the proportion of times reward occurs when a stimulus is present and the proportion of times it occurs when the stimulus is absent. Figure 8-4 was produced by simulating the effects of reward on behavior using only the simple model of expectation of reward present in RAT RACE 1. The top plot in Figure 8-4 was generated using a procedure where, for example, the green light plus the runway was reinforced 80 percent of the time and the red light plus the runway was never reinforced. In the middle plot, the green light plus the runway was reinforced 80 percent of the time and the red light plus the runway 80 percent of the time. In this case, there is no correlation between stimuli and reward and the expectation of reward in the presence of the green light is 0. In the bottom plot, green light plus runway was never reinforced and red light plus runway was reinforced 80 percent of the time. In this case, the expectation of reward associated with the green light is negative and the correlation between the green light and reward is negative. Such procedures can be simulated using program RAT'S ALLEY— that is, the simulated rat behaves as if it is sensitive to the correlation between stimuli and rewards.

Superstition

In many human situations, the opportunities to learn discriminations are rare. Severe droughts happen infrequently, and opportunities to learn effective behavior in those situations are therefore infrequent. Consider, for example, a farmer experiencing a severe drought. He hires a group of people to perform a rain dance, and it soon rains. The rain is followed by improvements in his crop yields, clearly a reward. The next year, there are large amounts of rain but he hires the group to do the rain dance "just in case." His yield does not increase.

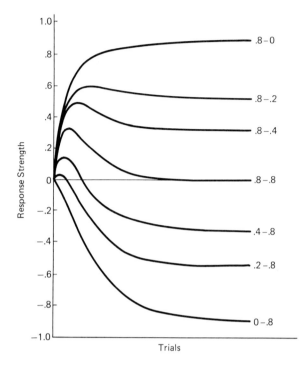

Figure 8-4.   Graph of sensitivity of behavior to the correlation between stimuli and reinforcers. The vertical axis is response strength. Numbers on the right are the probability of a reward in the presence or absence of the stimulus. When reward is equally likely in the presence or absence of a stimulus (0.8 – 0.8), for example, response strength will eventually (after large numbers of experiences) go to zero. (Abraham H. Black, William F. Prokasy, *Classical Conditioning II: Current Theory and Research,* ©1972, p. 89. Reprinted by permission of Prentice-Hall, Inc., Englewood Cliffs, N.J.)

In the first year, the rain dance appeared to increase crop yields in the presence of the drought condition, but the second year it did not result in increased yields in the presence of rain. We might expect the rain dance to have been equally rewarded and nonrewarded and therefore unlikely to occur in the future. Yet the common stimulus, in this case the crop, has large associative strength and we can predict that the farmer will hire the rain dance in the third year—no matter what the weather conditions. Since crop growing is an annual affair, people have only limited experience with it, and we would expect to see a lot of behavior surrounding farming that derives from a small number of experiences. We might call these kinds of behavior superstitious. As we see in program RAT'S ALLEY, the effects of initial rewards produce large changes in behavior that occur under the identical or common stimulus mediated conditions.

Fortunately, culture and science allow for the accumulation of experience by many individuals and across many lifetimes. Scientists gather observations about the behavior of many farmers and the crop yields they enjoy. They amalgamate these observations and report them to other farmers. Culturally developed methods of communication are used to transmit their information to other farmers through magazines, newspapers, books, radio, TV, and word-of-mouth. Much of this information is stored in documents for transmission from generation to generation. By refining this stored information about the conditions under which rewards occur, many superstitious behaviors are eliminated. This process ultimately leads us to be able to detect what stimuli are perfect predictors of reward. We call these stimuli *causes*. The detection of causes, or invariant temporal sequences of events, is a product of discrimination learning.

APPLICATIONS OF PROGRAM RAT'S ALLEY

No new applications of Artificial Behavior are suggested by program RAT'S ALLEY, only refinements of applications suggested in earlier chapters. RAT'S ALLEY can be used in educational settings to simulate many of the principles developed in the study of discrimination learning—the extent to which situational stimuli can enhance elation and depression, the effects of common cues in discrimination situations, blocking, and the effects of early rewards in producing behavior even in inappropriate settings. Simulations of discrimination learning illustrate the power of simple principles to describe complex behavior.

Computer gaming applications of AB stand to benefit substantially from incorporating the situational specificity of behavior simulated by program RAT'S ALLEY. In previous chapters, I talked about a knight in an animated computer adventure game who picked up rocks to find notes containing clues to help him rescue the princess. A believable game, however, requires that behavior to be situation specific. If he simply picked up things at a high frequency he might, when he finds the princess, simply pick her up and look under her. That behavior must be associated with rocks to create a good computer game. When this situational specificity of behavior is incorporated in the interactive graphics simulations discussed in previous chapters, behavior would change with the situation. Game characters would begin to show patterns of behavior more closely resembling that of real humans.

SUMMARY

It is a common observation that behavior is situation specific. People bowl in bowling alleys and read in libraries. The AB programs in previous chapters did not accommodate this situational specificity of behavior because they kept the situation constant. The model of behavior change used in those programs, however, assumes that behavior is associated with situations (stimuli). In this chapter, program RAT'S ALLEY was developed. This program simulates a rat running a runway for food. The situation always includes the runway and may or may not include a red light and a green light. The simulation requires the program to keep track of a matrix of psychological effects of rewards (expectations, frustration, and courage), and situations (runway, red light, and green light). Program RAT'S ALLEY can be used to simulate discrimination learning (reward only occurs in specific situations and not in others), the sensitivity of organisms to correlations between situations and reward, and superstitious behavior. Incorporating the situational specificity of behavior into AB yields programs that "react differently to different situations." Such programs are more likely to create "the illusion of personality."

REFERENCES

The idea of situational specificity of the effects of reward on behavior has a long history in philosophy and psychology. The first of these references is a textbook that emphasizes the situational specificity of learned behavior. The second reference surveys approximately fifty years of research on dicrimination learning.

1. Hill, W. F., *Principles of Learning: A Handbook of Applications* (Palo Alto, Calif.: Mayfield Publishing, 1982).
2. Sutherland, N. S., and MacKintosh, N. J., *Mechanisms of Animal Discrimination Learning* (New York: Academic Press, 1971).

9

FUTURE DIRECTIONS IN ARTIFICIAL BEHAVIOR

Programs RAT RACE, RAT 1, PIGEON 1, and RAT'S ALLEY demonstrate how psychological states such as expectation, frustration, depression, resistance to change, persistence, spontaneity, choice, discrimination, and superstition are produced by the relationships between behavior and its consequences. Each of these programs simulates different procedural details to help the user learn about the simulation of particular psychological states.

Program RAT'S ALLEY contains a single organism and a single behavior but three different situational variables. The different stimuli allow the program user to study the way in which the effects of situational variables interact with reward and nonreward to modify behavior. Program RAT 2 contains a constant situation but two behaviors. This program focuses attention on the effects of rewards on two or more behaviors in the same individual. Program RAT RACE focuses on comparisons of the effects of rewards and nonrewards on two different individuals. All of these programs incorporate simple rules describing the relationship between behavior and its consequences.

Changes in behavior often are a function of the difference between obtained rewards and expected rewards. When reward is greater than expected, expectations increase. When reward is less than expected, frustration increases. If reward occurs when frustration is expected, courage is acquired. The strength of any behavior is equal to the expectation of reward, minus the frustration, plus the courage acquired. Additional complexities in behavior arise from interactions of these rules in a variety of behaviors, a variety of situations, and a variety of individual reinforcement histories. The power of the model is great, but this power is difficult to grasp without noting that the psychological model is constant across these programs. The different programs illustrate the operation of the model when situations, behaviors, experimental procedures, and individual histories of reward vary.

All of the programs described and illustrated in this book are written in Applesoft BASIC. They can be typed into your Apple II series computer and stored to a tape or disk. Anyone with some familiarity with the BASIC language can understand how these programs work. Programmers familiar with more advanced graphics techniques, some knowledge of memory management, and knowledge of disk operating systems can use the AB techniques and ideas presented in this book to create more advanced programs.

Figure 9-1 illustrates the combination of the psychological model, a variety of behaviors, and a variety of situations. Behaviors are represented by rows in the matrix, situations are represented by columns, and the psychological constructs are represented by the third dimension. This is the matrix that would have to be maintained if we simulated a rat in a Skinner Box with two levers to

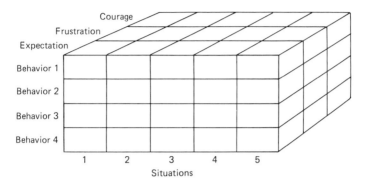

Figure 9-1. Three-dimensional matrix for storing values in a simulation with four different behaviors, five different situations, and the three psychological constructs in DMOD. This matrix may be repeated for different characters in a multi-individual simulation. It also can be repeated for entirely different scenes containing different behaviors and different situations in computer games and interactive fiction.

press, two chains to pull, three different colored lights, and two different tones. Such a simulation might contain a food dispenser and a water dispenser. The program user could turn the lights and tones off and on by keyboard inputs, and deliver food and water rewards to the rat. Such a simulation would produce complex patterns of behavior. It is highly unlikely that the simulation user could predict the behavior of the rat while the program was running.

The same matrix could be used to simulate human behavior. The scene might be an apartment with a view of the living room, kitchen, and dining area. The behaviors might be sitting in an easy chair, sitting at the dining room table, walking out the door, and visiting with other people. The situations might be the presence or absence of two friends, the presence or absence of the character's mother, food on the table or no food on the table, the time on the clock (5 P.M. or 10 P.M.), and the weather (calm or stormy) as seen through a window. The reinforcers could be such things as food to eat, smiles by the character's friends or mother, or watching television. The program user could control the presence or absence of the food, the facial expressions of the friends or mother, and turning on or off the TV. Manipulation of these conditions could be accomplished by keyboard input.

Facial expressions of the animated character could vary by writing a routine to express surprise whenever $O - E$ is large and then switching to happiness if it is a positive quantity or sadness if it is a negative quantity. When the character expects to be frustrated, he might express fear.

Such a program would work very much like RAT'S ALLEY and RAT 2. Whenever a behavior occurred, the program would calculate the changes in expectancy, frustration, and courage depending upon the occurrence or nonoccurrence of reward and the situational variables. After those new values were stored in the matrix, the program would begin its pass through the matrix of behaviors and situations, generating random numbers and comparing them to the response strength for each behavior. Whenever the random number was less than the response strength, the behavior would occur. All the while, the program user could reward or not reward behavior, and change situational variables, all through keyboard inputs.

In principle, there is no reason why such a simulation must be limited to one animated character. Two or more characters could be animated and a separate matrix of behaviors by situations by response strengths could be maintained for each character. This, of course, would make for a very exciting simulation. Humans are very social animals. Contact with one another and such things as facial expressions during those interactions are powerful sources of social approval and disapproval (i.e., rewards). In a simulation with more than one animated character, the behavior that brings one character close to another one will produce reward. In this case, the behavior producing the reward would no longer be under the direct control of the program user, but would arise as a consequence of the execution of the program itself.

There is no reason why such a simulation must be limited to only one scene (the living room/kitchen/dining area, for example). If the animated character walked out the door, the program could store the matrices of response strengths for all characters in that scene on the disk and load into the computer the graphics and matrices for another scene. The other scene might include other characters. Common variables could be passed between scenes. These techniques could be used to write computer soap operas, games, or interactive fiction.

The psychological principles and programming techniques developed in Chapters 2 through 8 of this book can be used to write elaborate simulation programs with reasonable assurance that they will mimic many aspects of real human behavior.

It is clear that the trend in computer hardware of increased computing power per dollar will continue in the immediate future. There seems little doubt that we can expect 32-bit machines with at least one megabyte of RAM memory and large amounts of peripheral storage at price ranges equivalent to the cost of many of today's home, business, and educational systems. What use we will make of these machines is less clear. Artificial Behavior offers an approach for new uses of computers for research, education, gaming, fiction, operating systems, and robotics.

FUTURE APPLICATIONS OF ARTIFICIAL BEHAVIOR

Research Applications

Computer simulation has been an important research tool for many years. In fact, the development of computers has a history of a close interaction with their use as a simulation device. The United States Department of Defense was crucially involved in the early development of these machines to use as number crunchers and simulators for research in artillery and ballistics. Simulation of weather phenomena also has motivated hardware and software development. The psychological use of computer simulation has, for the most part, been limited to the field of Artificial Intelligence.

The AI approach, as described in Chapter 1, is concerned with patterns of behavior once they are well established. These patterns of behavior are typically described as strategies, traits, and characteristics. The experimental analysis of behavior has as its task the explanation of how organisms acquire discriminations, expectations, and all such fundamental units that operate to produce strategies, traits, characteristics of personality, emotion, and intelligence. Even though experimental psychologists have uncovered many processes that they claim are capable of providing the building blocks for explaining intelligent behavior, the bridge between the two approaches has rarely been attempted. Computer simulation provides a tool for constructing that bridge. Complex AB programs can be run for long periods of time to see if the characters in them develop patterns of behavior similar to human strategies, traits, and characteristics.

Researchers might wish to create AB programs that yield strip charts, bar charts, or cumulative records as outputs instead of animated pictures of the behaving organisms. These graphs could then be compared to graphs prepared from the behavior of real individuals to test the fit of a formal model to an actual behaving individual. Such procedures are now common in the AI field and are having substantial payoffs in the development of "expert systems" for a wide variety of applications. The use of such techniques in Artificial Behavior could lead to the development of electronic organisms, an issue to be discussed at some length under Robotic Applications.

The use of AB techniques can lead to a rapid increase in the refinement of basic knowledge in experimental psychology. It also could help with the construction of engineering bridges between basic research and complex phenomena in social psychology, intelligence, personality, politics, sociology, and other social sciences.

Educational Applications

Many research findings in cognitive psychology and learning seem so trivial that they are easily forgotten. It is well known, for example, that learning is more rapid and more enduring if the student is actively involved (behaving) in the learning process. Passive, silent rehearsal (self-talk or thinking) produces only very weak learning. Have you ever considered learning to ride a bicycle by thinking about it, or reading about it? Bicycle riding, which is most frequently learned by doing, is something that is easy to relearn. Knowing how to ride a bicycle, once learned, seems never to go away. Most education about human behavior is, on the other hand, commonly conducted by assigning reading, lecturing, and so on—forms of activity that are known to produce weak learning. This is particularly evident in areas such as sociology, political science, psychology, anthropology, and history. On the other hand, laboratory exercises are common in the physical sciences such as physics, chemistry, and engineering. Actually doing the activity with paper and pencil is common with basic skills such as spelling and mathematics. In the behavioral sciences, few students ever directly modify behavior, dig anthropological relics, observe evolutionary products, or participate in political processes. There are many reasons for this deficiency, but one important one is expense. Only a small number of anthropology students are actively involved in their subject matter because of the expenses of travel, supervision, tools, and housing. Similar expenses are a problem in psychology. Animal behavior laboratories are expensive to build, equip, and maintain. Computer simulation offers students a tool for active involvement with lifelike subject matter.

For example, the June 1984 issue of BYTE contains an article on a simulation of a heart that can be used to study the operation of its chambers and variables such as volume and pressure. Apple Computer, Inc., has always provided a copy of the business simulation Lemonade Stand to purchasers of the APPLE II series of computers. Other business simulations are widely used in high schools, colleges, and universities because of their ability to get students actively involved in the subject matter. No one claims that such programs are perfect replicas of the real world. They work because they embody some of our knowledge and because they get students actively involved. The programs in this book are similar in that they embody much existing knowledge and require the program user to behave. The program user obtains feedback about the relationship between behavior and its consequences.

There are reasons other than expense for not allowing behavioral science students more active involvement with their subject matter. Use of animals for educational purposes is considered by many to be unethical. The use of humans as research subjects in behavioral sciences presents even larger ethical problems, problems that could be avoided if we were to develop more educational computer simulations in the behavioral sciences. They are cost-effective, present few ethical dilemmas, and get students involved in lifelike examples of their subject matter when they use graphics animation.

General Psychological Applications

At the beginning of Chapter 2, I discussed the fact that many children and adults can learn useful skills at recognizing and naming facial expressions using the program FACES. When facial expressions of emotion are combined with the rules by which behavior is related to its consequences, program users can learn what situations give rise to various emotions. These rules apply to ourselves as well as others. The self-help industry has become so large that it provides ample testimony to the desire that many people have to understand themselves. Programs that simulate psychological processes can be designed to help people make observations of their behavior and its consequences. These observations can be used to help people understand their behavior and institute behavior-change activities when they wish.

As our knowledge of psychology has grown, it has become increasingly obvious that we are not well designed to know ourselves. Self-observation consists predominately of private verbal behavior (thinking, meditation, reflection). We are very visual organisms, but our eyes are not designed so that we can watch ourselves. It is difficult for us to speak and listen to ourselves simultaneously. As behavioral approaches to psychology have become increasingly more effective, therapists have been looking for new ways to obtain observations of the naturally occurring behaviors of their clients. We now give paper-and-pencil tests in which we ask someone "How might you behave in this or that situation?" One of the weaknesses of these tests is that the person's verbal report may or may not accurately reflect how they would behave in a given situation. Alternatively, we could have the client use an interactive computer simulation and the machine could make a record of how they would behave in a given situation. To the extent that the simulation is realistic, we would no longer have to rely on the client's verbal conjecture but could observe his or her actual behavior in the simulated situation. This is a diagnostic, role playing application of AB. We also might use simulations for teaching by playing one of the animated characters and noting the consequences of various behaviors.

With increasing frequency, therapists are having their clients gather daily observations of their behavior and their environments. These observations are then reviewed by the therapist and the client to try to identify the situations in which particular behaviors occur and what the consequences are of maintaining the behaviors. Most people could learn to gather these observations and then run simulation programs to confirm or disconfirm their hypotheses about what is maintaining their behavior. They could then run simulations to test "what-if" questions regarding changes they might want to make in their behavior.

Computer Games and Interactive Fiction Applications

Adventure games typically are designed so that the game player participates as a character in the game. When you sit down to play The Wizard and the Princess, it is your task to find your way through an environment that you can manipulate with verbal commands. The most complicated difficulty you encounter involves a programmer's conditional branching routines. A bridge may not appear over a chasm, for example, unless you first find two pieces of a note containing a magic word, figure out what the word is, and type it into the computer. The game programmer has presented you with a complex game environment. These games are very lifelike because your behavior is being affected by the complexity of the game environment. In playing the game, you develop expectations, become frustrated, and show other psychological effects. However, these adventure games are not lifelike machines; they are merely complex environments that affect your life.

Artificial Behavior suggests a different type of adventure game. Imagine a game of The Wizard and the Princess that starts out with an animated knight on the screen. The knight has a repertoire of behaviors programmed to occur randomly and at low frequencies (similar to RAT 1, RAT 2, and PIGEON 1). You have control over the screen environment. Your task is to manipulate the relationship between environmental events and the knight's behavior so that he acquires the appropriate patterns of behavior needed to find and rescue the princess. Let's say, for example, that pressing the N key makes notes appear. The knight looks into the hole in the tree and you push the N key. If notes have been specified by the programmer to function as rewards, the program would then calculate an increase in the knight's expectation to find notes in trees. Of course, if you gave the knight some particular sequence of rewards for looking in trees, you might produce a knight who so persistently looked inside of trees that he missed opportunities to engage in other behaviors that must occur in order for him to find and rescue the Princess. In the process of playing the game, the knight's patterns of behavior would be changing continuously. The knight's behavior would change as a function of its consequences. You, the game player, would have control over the environmental events that served as consequences. Every time the game was started anew, a new character would develop with his own patterns of behavior—his own personality. Perhaps the programmer designed the game so that only one particular pattern of behavior, one very special personality, was capable of rescuing the princess. Such a computer game can be developed using the techniques of Artificial Behavior presented in this book.

Integration of the algorithm for the facial expression of emotion (presented in Chapter 2), and the model of expectations, frustration, and courage from RAT RACE would make a more interesting game. Whenever rewards were larger than expected, the knight might show an expression of surprise. Whenever expectations dropped below the level appropriate to a reward (depression), the knight's expression might be one of sadness. Values of T4 (total expectation) larger than the maximum supportable by a reward (elation) might call the subroutine for the facial expression of happiness. Anger or fear expressions could be displayed whenever frustration was large. By pairing the behavior-generating routines of RAT RACE and the expressions of FACES, a computer adventure game could produce extremely versatile and life-like characters.

Artificial Behavior adventure games would have a number of interesting characteristics. First, they would define a new type of entertainment we might wish to call interactive fiction. Second, while in existing adventure games the player has direct access to a major character's behavior (himself), in AB adventure games the player has only indirect access to the major character's behavior. The player's access to the character's behavior is through his or her ability to manipulate relationships between behavior and its consequences. An AB game player would be learning about our knowledge of psychology while playing the game. Third, the animated character would represent a human-like machine. AB adventure games would be entertaining, educational, and serve as a vehicle for the creation of human-like machines.

Computer Operating Systems and Robotics Applications

Artificial Behavior techniques embody human-like psychological proc-esses into instruction sets for computers. The applications discussed thus far include education software, applied psychology, and computer gaming. There is no reason, however, why the rules describing psychological processes cannot be incorporated into the software governing the operating characteristics of the machine (operating systems). One important consideration is that the machine be constantly supplied with electrical current or contain nonvolatile memory. Since both of these are available, I will assume that one of those conditions is present in our machines.

Imagine a computer that contained the model describing the acquisition of expectations, frustration, and courage programmed into its operating system. If we defined user time, a priori, as a desirable consequence, the computer would become depressed if we changed from using it six hours a day to using it only thirty minues a day. It might then ask us why we didn't like it anymore. We might feel compelled to use it more frequently in order to maintain the relationship and to avoid hurting the machine's feelings. The operating system could develop expectations about what software we were most likely to use at particular times on particular days. The computer would then automatically load that software. We would have to tell our computer friend what we wanted to do only if it were different from the computer's expectations. But then it might tell us that it expected to do word processing and therefore didn't feel like doing a financial ledger.

We also have models in psychology for such things as self-control. Imagine the consequences of building a model of self-control into our computer's operating system. Our computer might tell us something like, "John, I have to quit playing games now. I have to be ready to run Mary's self-observation program in forty-five minutes and I still have some charts and graphs to prepare for her." It would then disable our input devices.

Such operating system applications are currently possible using available rules describing psychological processes.

Current computers have limited repertoires of behavior. They can print to a video monitor or printer. They can, with some assistance, speak. They can write to magnetic surfaces, and with help, operate other electrical devices. They also have limited sensory receptivity—mice, keyboards, joysticks, graphics tablets, and so on. The field of robotics is extending the behavioral repertoire of machines to more human-like activities of grasping, locomoting, turning, and generally all manner of movement in three dimensional space. Robotics is extending the sensory reception domain to include human-like sensitivities to light, sound, touch, temperature, and so on. Obviously, pairing the AB techniques presented in this book with current technology from robotics can produce very human-like machines.

We currently envision robots that brew our morning coffee, serve it beside our bed, and then turn on our electronic news device. However, we all know that we would have to tell the robot what time we want those services. Imagine instead a robot that could learn what time to expect us to wake up. We would only have to tell it about changes or exceptions to our routines (sound familiar?). Imagine a grass-cutting robot that could learn when the grass needed to be cut and what movements to make to cut it efficiently. We currently think of these characteristics as ones we would have to program explicitly into the robot. I am suggesting instead that we imbed into the robot a set of rules that would allow it to acquire expectations, frustration, and courage, similar to those progammed into RAT RACE.

The use of Artificial Behavior techniques would give us robots that not only had minds of their own but feelings as well. Their expectations could be violated, generating frustration, which in turn could produce behavioral consequences such as aggression. Robots could be harmed and become afraid—and then run away from home. Their fears could be reduced, generating relief. All of this is possible with existing knowledge and technology.

SOME CLOSING WORDS

Many of the speculations contained in this chapter may seem like science fiction. What I am saying is that we can develop artificial, behaving organisms that show many psychological characteristics similar to our own. That claim has, of course, been made before. Many would say that the scientific community has cried wolf too often. The evidence is quite the contrary. AI researchers said they could develop an outstanding medical diagnostic computer, chess player, and weather forecaster, and they have. Medical researchers said they could develop an artificial heart, and they did. Molecular biologists claimed they could engineer genetically new organisms, and they did. Embryologists claimed they could fertilize a human egg outside of a uterus, and they did. We have created artificial organs, artificial organisms, and artificial intelligence. In a very real sense, none of these are artificial. They are products of our own scientific evolution. A scientific analysis of psychology now suggests Artificial Behavior. The eight programs in this book are rudimentary examples. In only a few short years, Artificial Behavior will give us simulations that are in many particulars indistinguishable from humans. Science, a cultural phenomenon, leads us to increasingly more accurate models of ourselves.

ADDITIONAL READINGS

1. Dennett, D. C., "Why the Law of Effect Will Not Go Away," *Journal of the Theory of Social Behavior,* 1975, *5,* 169–87.

2. Selmi, P. M., Klein, M. H., Greist, J. H., Johnson, J. H., and Harris, W. G., "An Investigation of Computer-Assisted Cognitive-Behavior Therapy in the Treatment of Depression," *Behavior Research Methods and Instrumentation,* 1982, *14,* 181–85.

3. Castellan, N. J., "Computers in Psychology: A Survey of Instructional Applications," *Behavioral Research Methods and Instrumentation,* 1982, *14,* 198–202.

4. Staats, A. W., and Burns, G. L., "Intelligence and Child Development: What Intelligence Is and How It Is Learned and Functions," *Genetic Psychology Monographs,* 1981, *104,* 237–301.

10

MORE PSYCHOLOGICAL PHENOMENA FOR SIMULATION

Psychologists have developed laboratory procedures for studying numerous psychological processes and states. Some of these procedures are quite simple, such as the procedure for studying generalization, and some are very complex, such as the procedure for studying the nature of reward. In a few cases, as in the study of mate selection, mathematical models have been developed that describe large amounts of research. In other cases, well-defined experimental procedures have been developed (such as in the study of lying).

A list follows of eight psychological phenomena that you will find interesting to simulate. Artificial Behavior programs can be readily developed for each of these phenomena. Each psychological construct has a brief description and a reference from the scientific literature that contains sufficient information to get you started on developing a simulation.

SELF-CONTROL

Self-control has been of considerable interest to researchers in recent years. Briefly, it involves the interaction of short-term and long-term rewards and the effects of self-verbalizations on other behavior. Self-control requires that behavior that yields short-term rewards must not occur, and behavior that yields long-term rewards must increase. We have been able to teach self-control to laboratory animals and to humans by providing them with behavioral options (under stimulus control) for bridging the time between short-term and long-term rewards. An excellent summary and discussion of these research and applied procedures is found in the following book chapter.

Catania, A. C., and Brigham, T. A. *Handbook of Applied Behavior Analysis,* Chapter 8, "Self-control," pp. 206–74. (New York: Irvington Publishers, 1978).

GENERALIZATION

One of the most important empirical facts in psychology is the observation that if a rat is running fast when a red light is on, he will run faster when an orange light is present than when a yellow light is present. The more similar a situation is to the original learning situation, the stronger the behavior. If you meet someone new and they look like and act like your grandmother, your own behavior will be similar to what it is around your grandmother. If the new person looks and acts like one of your friends, your own behavior will be similar to what it is around your friends.

Generalization is a powerful and complex phenomenon. It has been widely studied since the pioneering work of Pavlov in the early decades of this century. Generalization will be an important component of our eventual understanding of such complex behaviors as concept formation. It is the basis for demonstrating similarity, analogy, and variability in the situational specificity of behavior discussed in Chapter 8. You should be warned, however, that this is a complex phenomenon. An accurate model of generalization will eventually depend upon a full understanding of human sensory systems and human perception. It is possible, however, to develop good Artificial Behavior simulations that demonstrate generalization using existing knowledge. The following two references contain formal models of generalization and discrimination.

Blough, D. A., "Steady-State Data and a Quantitative Model of Operant Generalization and Discrimination," *Journal of Experimental Psychology: Animal Behavior Processes,* 1975, *104,* 3–21.

Kendler, T. S., Basden, B. H., and Bruckner, J. B., "Dimensional Dominance and Continuity Theory, " *Journal of Experimental Psychology,* 1970, *83,* 309–18.

FEAR, PUNISHMENT

This book has dealt only with the laws relating behavior and desirable consequences. Many behaviors are modified by undesirable consequences. For instance, behaviors sometimes decrease in frequency because they have been followed by punishment. The analysis of punishment and fear has been more difficult than the analysis of expectations of reward. It is possible that the effects of adverse consequences are described by a set of rules that are symmetrical but opposite from those in DMOD. One difficulty arises from the fact that with rewards separate events define a motivational state—i.e., the rat is food deprived. With punishment, the punisher both induces the motivational state and serves as the reinforcer. If you are interested in simulating aversively motivated behavior, first try the symmetrical DMOD suggestion. Next, you might want to read some of the chapters in the following book.

Campbell, B. A., and Church, R. M., *Punishment and Aversive Behavior* (New York: Appleton-Century-Crofts, 1969).

MATE SELECTION

This is a topic of interest to most people. Any computer simulation of mate selection, or any interactive game that incorporated our knowledge of mate selection, might be a best-seller. In 1972, Robert Trivers, a biologist, published a formalization of observations of mate selection in many species. His formalization is known as *Parental Investment Theory*. This theory is the topic of much continuing research in behavioral biology. Briefly, Parental Investment Theory says that individuals will be guided in their mate selection by their investments in offspring. Stability of mating relationships will depend on the relative investments each partner makes in offspring or potential offspring. The partner with the larger investment will always be under the threat of desertion. A computer simulation of this area would be intriguing.

Trivers, R. L., "Parental Investment and Sexual Selection," in B. Campbell (ed.), *Sexual Selection and the Descent of Man* (Chicago: Aldine, 1972).

VERBAL BEHAVIOR

Many psychologists still observe that the unique defining characteristic of the human species is language behavior. Behavioral psychologists have long argued that language, as any other behavior, is modified by its consequences. There are now many empirical demonstrations that it is. Research on the modification of verbal behavior by its consequences is now spread across a large number of fields—linguistics, psycholinguistics, education, and child development, to name only a few. Anyone interested in the simulation of language behavior would do well to read Skinner's treatment of the subject and then return to Chapters Three to Eight of this book.

Skinner, B. F., *Verbal Behavior* (Englewood Cliffs, N.J. Prentice-Hall, Inc., 1957).

REWARD

The simulation programs presented in this book are of simple laboratory preparations. In those procedures, animals are food deprived for a limited number of hours. This serves to make food rewarding. It is more difficult in complex natural settings to determine what events serve as rewards. One solution to this problem, suggested by David Premack in the late 1960s, simply identifies high-frequency behaviors as rewards. Food is an effective reward for a hungry rat because the rat spends a lot of time eating. This idea is known as the Premack Principle. It has enjoyed enormous success in education and behavior therapy settings. It also recognizes the individual nature of the answer to the question, what's a reward? According to the Premack Principle that question can be answered by rank-ordering behaviors from high frequency to low frequency. Access to high-frequency behaviors (i.e., making food available to a hungry rat and driving many twelve-year-old children to the movie theatre) will reinforce low-frequency behavior. Playing baseball serves as a reinforcer when we tell a child "Yes, you can go play baseball if you make your bed and clean your room first." Access to baseball is reinforcing bed making and room cleaning. The Premack Principle is amenable to formalization and computer simulation. It also can be incorporated into AB games and fiction.

Premack, D., "Catching Up with Common Sense or Two Sides of a Generalization: Reinforcement and Punishment," in R. Glaser (ed.), *The Nature of Reinforcement* (New York: Academic Press, 1971).

COOPERATION

Many times in human affairs rewards depend upon the behaviors of more than one person. Those behaviors can operate to speed the receipt of rewards (cooperation) or can operate to impede their receipt. In these complex situations, two animated graphics characters are necessary for a successful simulation. There must be rewards that depend on the joint behavior of both characters. Procedures for studying cooperation that are useful for simulation can be found in the following book.

Catania, A. C., and Brigham, T. A., *Handbook of Applied Behavior Analysis,* Chapter 7, "Cooperation, Competition, and Related Social Phenomena" (New York: Irvington Publishers, 1978), pp. 208–45.

LYING

Among the more interesting recent endeavors of the experimental analysis of behavior has been the development of procedures for studying symbolic communication between pigeons, the use of memoranda by pigeons, and the study of lying in pigeons. The procedures are outlined in detail in the following articles.

Epstein, R., Lanza, R. P., and Skinner, B. F., "Symbolic Communication Between Two Pigeons," *Science,* 1980, *207,* 543–45.

Epstein, R., and Skinner, B. F., "The Spontaneous Use of Memoranda by Pigeons," *Behavior Analysis Letters,* 1981, *1,* 241–46.

Lanza, R. P., Starr, J., and Skinner, B. F., " 'Lying' in the Pigeon," *Journal of the Experimental Analysis of Behavior,* 1982, *38,* 201–03.

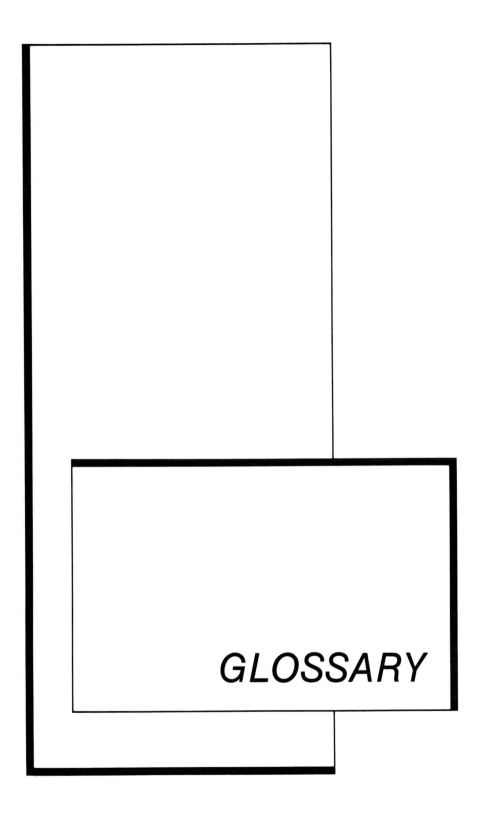

GLOSSARY

ADVENTURE GAME—computer program that presents a challenge to a user to solve some puzzle, such as discovering buried treasure, and then mimics the world by presenting obstacles and aids to solution. Examples are Mystery House, Zork, and The Wizard and The Princess.

ALGORITHM—method for solving a problem; a set of rules for going from a problem to a solution. An animation algorithm is any technique for producing the perception of motion by a set of rules for presenting an image at one screen location, removing it, and then presenting it at a new screen location in such a way that it appears to move.

ARTIFICIAL BEHAVIOR—behavior of a computer that simulates the behavior of an animal. The computer's behavior can be screen animation, operating system output, or robotics. The crucial point is that the behavior of the electronic system mimics the behavior of a real live organism in a changing environment.

ARTIFICIAL INTELLIGENCE—computer output that mimics complex rule governed or strategy based behavior of a human. Chess-playing programs and medical diagnosis programs are examples.

ASSOCIATION—hypothesized connection between two nervous system events. The association of environmental events and behavior is frequently assumed to account for the situational specificity of human behavior.

BLOCKING—in discrimination learning, when a person has learned that situation A predicts reward X, pairings of situation B and reward X will not produce learning about B if A is present. Since A already is known to predict reward, the person does not learn that B also predicts reward.

CHOICE—used to refer to behavior when there are two or more alternative behaviors available. If we are going to the movies, and there are two films available, which film we go to is choice behavior. If there is only one film to see, the immediate situation does not involve choice. Behavior in the context of other behavior.

CONCURRENT SCHEDULE—a laboratory procedure for studying choice. Two or more behaviors are simultaneously available, each with its own source of reward. A rat, for example, can pull a chain for water or press a lever for food.

CONTINUOUS REWARD—a situation in which every time a particular behavior occurs it is followed by reward. Contrast with Partial Reward, a situation in which a particular behavior is only occasionally rewarded.

COORDINATE—on a graph, the lines used to define new points on the graph. In computer graphics, the light pixels (light spots on the screen) are defined by their location on a pair of horizontal and vertical coordinates.

CORRELATION—an index of the extent two things change in unison. For people who are paid every Monday, there is a correlation between the day of the week and the amount of money they have. At the beginning of the week, they have larger amounts of money, and at the end of the week they have less money. The day of the week tells those people something about the amount of money they have available.

COURAGE—if a person is rewarded following a behavior when they expected to be frustrated, they learn to engage in the behavior even when experiencing a negative affect or emotion. Persistence in the face of expectation of frustration is called courage.

DEPRESSION—when a person experiences a reduction in reward amount from large to small, his or her behavior falls to a level below that which is normally produced by small reward. The fact that behavior falls to an unusually low level as a consequence of reward reduction is called depression.

DISCRIMINATION—when a person has learned that a particular behavior is followed by reward in one situation, but not followed by reward in a different situation, he has learned a discrimination. Bowling is rewarded by social approval in bowling alleys but not in church.

DMOD—the psychological model developed by Helen and John Daly. The model says three psychological processes, expectations, frustration, and courage change as a constant fraction of the discrepancy between obtained and expected consequences of behavior.

ELATION—increases from small to large rewards sometimes elevate behavior to a level greater than what is normally produced by large rewards. These are instances of elation.

EMOTION—refers to the physiological states, and a person's verbal labels for those states, which arise as a consequence of intense stimulation.

EXPECTATION—refers to increases in behavior which are followed by reward. If a behavior has been previously followed by reward, and now occurs quite vigorously, we summarize the past effects of reward in producing the vigorous behavior by saying the person has an expectation of reward.

FACIAL AFFECT SCORING TECHNIQUE (FAST)—a set of rules describing facial features. It can be used to identify facial expressions of surprise, fear, anger, disgust, sadness, and happiness. It can also be used as a research tool for studying other facial expressions.

FREEDOM—behavior that is unconstrained by procedures or conditions other than those imposed by the effects of the behavior's consequences (rewards and punishments). When an individual has many behaviors available we say the person enjoys a large measure of freedom.

FRUSTRATION—behavior that occurs when reward is not obtained but was expected. Frustration is known to result in behaviors categorized as aggression, regression, avoidance, persistence, etc.

INTERACTIVE—in this book, refers to computer programs that allow the program user's input to effect the output of the program. The user behaves and the computer output constantly changes as a function of the input. Since this is true of almost any computer program the specific use here is with regard to the interactive nature of the video display. The behavior of the animal on the screen depends on the behavior of the animal at the keyboard (the program user).

INTERACTIVE FICTION—interactive, animated computer programs with a variety of characters and scenes. Some of the events on the screen are under the control of the program user. The program user's manipulation of events effects the behaviors of the characters on the screen. The personalities of the characters develop, and the story unfolds, as a function of the behavior of the program user. The story is different each time the program is run.

LEARNING—changes in behavior which occur as a function of experience.

LEARNING CURVE—the amount of change in a behavior which occurs with each successive rewarded occurrence is smaller and smaller. A plot of the strength of behavior as a function of rewarded occurrences is negatively accelerated. This type of curve is also called one of diminishing returns. Instructions for making a learning curve are given in Chapter Three.

LOOP—a set of computer instructions which cause the machine to execute the set of instructions repeatedly. When the last instruction in the set is executed the computer returns to the first instruction and loops through the set of instructions again. In BASIC the FOR/NEXT command is used to write program loops.

MATCHING LAW—the amount of one behavior (A) divided by the total amount of all behaviors equals the amount of reward for behavior A divided by the total amount of all rewards.

MODEL—an imitation of something that does not contain all of the dimensions, or their values, of the thing being imitated. A model airplane. A model of behavior.

OPERATING SYSTEM—a set of instructions governing the interaction of all of the parts of a computer system and the user. LOAD, RUN, and CATALOG are, for example, operating system commands. When no programs are loaded into the computer's memory the operating system governs the behavior of the computer.

PARTIAL REWARD—a situation in which only some occurrences of a behavior are followed by reward. Partial reward produces persistent behavior. This fact is known to psychologists as the partial reinforcement extinction effect.

PERSISTENCE—the repeated occurrence of a behavior long after all sources of reward have stopped.

PIXEL—the smallest space on your TV screen, or computer monitor, to which light can be applied. Individual pixel's are identified by their location on a set of coordinates.

RANDOM NUMBER—a number that is selected from a pool of numbers in such a way that all of the numbers in the pool are equally likely to be selected.

RESISTANCE TO CHANGE—refers to the ease with which behaviors can be eliminated and then replaced by some new behavior.

REWARD—an event which increases the strength of the behavior that it follows. For hungry animals, food functions as a reward. For thirsty animals water functions as a reward.

ROBOTICS—the science of building electromechanical machines that move in three dimensional space. They move, reach, grasp, etc. under their own control.

RUNWAY—a simple apparatus for studying the running behavior of rats in a laboratory. Typically four to six feet in length, three or four inches wide, and six inches tall. A runway is modeled in program RAT RACE. It contains a start box, run section, and a goal box.

SELECTION BY CONSEQUENCES—the general idea that in evolution, psychology, and culture, life is modified by events that follow its expression. In psychology it refers to the increase in behaviors that are rewarded and the decrease in behaviors that are punished.

SELF-CONTROL—when a person forsakes short term rewards in favor of doing things that obtain longer term rewards we say they show self control. Self control can be produced by environmental events (stimuli) which signal progress towards long term goals.

SIMULATION—to have many of the characteristics of some process without actually being the complete thing. Apple Computer's game Lemonade Stand simulates the operation of a road side commercial lemonade-selling venture. Computer simulation refers to the use of a computer to simulate or mimic real-world processes.

SKINNER BOX—a simple, highly controlled laboratory environment for conducting research on the effects of reward on behavior. Developed by B. F. Skinner and now commercially manufactured for behavioral research.

SOFTWARE—a set of instructions that tell a computer what to do. Also known as a computer program.

SPONTANEITY—behavior that occurs in the absence of any easy to identify stimulation. The initial lever press in a Skinner Box (and in Programs RAT 1, RAT 2, and PIGEON 1) is labeled as spontaneous because no information is available about how or why it occurs. This does not mean that it is not possible to explain its occurrence, but rather that it is not possible to explain its occurrence on the basis of available information.

STIMULUS—an environmental event that impinges on a person's sensory system. When the light goes on in a room, the light is a stimulus. Stimuli are important in the explanation of the situational specificity of behavior.

STIMULUS CONTROL—situational specificity of behavior is described in psychology by saying that behavior is controlled by stimuli. Many behaviors only occur under very specific environmental conditions. The study of changes in stimulus control that occur as a function of reward led to the development of DMOD, the psychological model used in many of the programs in this book.

SUBSCRIPT—when we have a number of things that are all to be treated the same, we assign them numbers. In program RAT 2, lever pressing is called $B(1)$ and chain pulling is called $B(2)$. B stands for behavior and the numbers 1 and 2 are subscripts representing lever pressing (1) and chain pulling (2).

SUPERSTITION—after small amounts of experience with reward, before discriminations are well developed, it is common to behave as if some inappropriate stimulus is a perfect predictor of reward. An example is provided in Chapter 8 of how small amounts of experience may lead a farmer to hire raindancers as a superstitious behavior.

SUBROUTINE—a portion of a computer program that carries out a part of the total task the program does. In a financial spreadsheet program, there might be a subroutine to prepare graphs. In the AB programs in this book, animation is carried out by subroutines.

TOTAL EXPECTATION—in DMOD, expectation of reward, minus frustration, plus courage.

TRIAL—a discrete unit of experience that includes some stimulus conditions, a behavior, and some outcome. A rat running a runway and then obtaining food is a trial.

VERBAL BEHAVIOR—behaviors of writing, speaking, and thinking that involve symbols which represent real world events. Verbal behavior, like other forms of behavior, is modified by its consequences.

ARTIFICIAL BEHAVIOR PROGRAMS ON DISK

All of the programs in this book are available on a single floppy disk. Save yourself the effort of typing them into your machine. All programs are unprotected BASIC, exactly as they appear in the text of this book.

Please check which computer you use.

_____ APPLE II

_____ IBM

_____ ATARI 800

Enclose $20.00 per disk, and $2.50 shipping & handling. California residents include 6% sales tax. Price subject to change.

YOUR NAME _____

YOUR ADDRESS _____

CITY _____

STATE AND ZIP CODE _____

Mail your order to:

Artificial Behavior, Inc.
4974 N. Fresno, Suite 326
Fresno, CA 93726

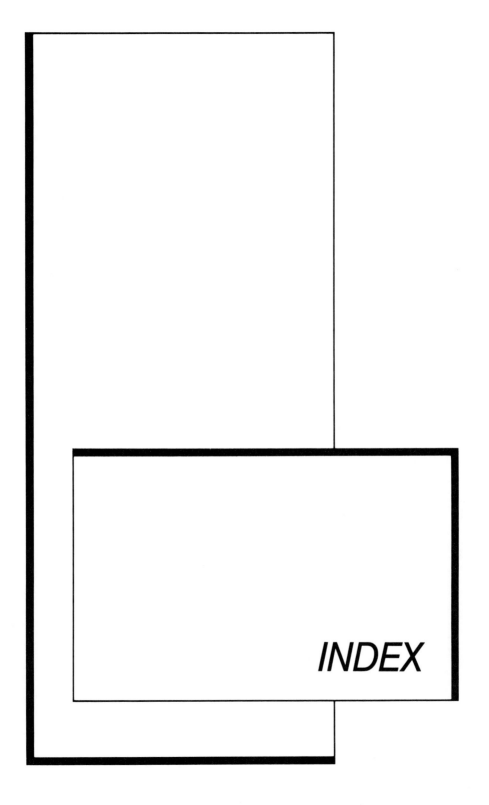

INDEX